'Smethurst is a compassionat[e] ... a unique angle of the war t[o] ... by men on the front line.'
Jessie Tu

'*The Freedom Circus* has a cinematic quality, as the narrative pans across several continents while Smethurst creates a sharp contrast between the horrors unfurling outside the Big Top world and the high-octane stunts and escapism inside it. It is an extraordinary wartime story of survival, escape and ingenuity.'
Weekend Australian

'There's plenty to nourish us in *The Freedom Circus*, where we have Sue Smethurst's persistence to thank. She cajoled her grandmother-in-law (with cakes from St Kilda) into telling her the story of her escape from Poland and across much of the world.'
Australian Jewish News

'An enthralling tale of survival against the odds. Readers will find themselves totally caught up in the fate of Mindla and her family.'
Canberra Times

'Bubbling with memorable details, *The Freedom Circus* is an astonishing and compelling read.'
Reading's Summer Reading Guide

PENGUIN BOOKS

THE
FREEDOM
CIRCUS

Sue Smethurst is an award-winning author and journalist who has spent more than twenty years working in the media across television, radio and magazines. She is currently a senior writer with *The Australian Women's Weekly* and has written eight books, including *Behind Closed Doors, Spartacus and Me, Blood on the Rosary* and *A Diamond in the Dust.*

THE
FREEDOM
CIRCUS

One family's death-defying act
to escape the Nazis and start
a new life in Australia

SUE SMETHURST

PENGUIN BOOKS

PENGUIN BOOKS

UK | USA | Canada | Ireland | Australia
India | New Zealand | South Africa | China

Penguin Books is part of the Penguin Random House group of companies
whose addresses can be found at global.penguinrandomhouse.com.

Penguin
Random House
Australia

First published by Ebury Press, 2020
This edition first published by Penguin Books, 2021

Cover photography: street in Warsaw Jewish Ghetto © Photo 12 / Alamy Stock Photo;
family © Halinskyi Maksym / Shutterstock.com; balloon © Cryptographer / Shutterstock.
com; blue strokes to make Star of David © Anastasia Shemetova / Shutterstock.com
Cover design by Adam Laszczuk © Penguin Random House Australia
Text design by Midland Typesetters, Australia
Typeset in Bembo by Midland Typesetters, Australia
Printed and bound in Australia by Griffin Press, part of Ovato, an accredited
ISO ANZ/NZS 14001 Environmental Management Systems printer

A catalogue record for this
book is available from the
National Library of Australia

ISBN 978 1 76089 032 2

penguin.com.au

MIX
Paper from
responsible sources
FSC® C009448

For Nanna and Zaydee. For those who made it to the Lucky Country and those who never had the chance. We will never forget.

CONTENTS

Part III: After the War

PROLOGUE

'Here comes the princess, always dressed for a ball,' the nurse affectionately said to my grandmother-in-law as we passed in the corridors of the Montefiore Jewish nursing home.

Mindla (pronounced *Marnya*) Horowitz. The Princess of Montefiore. Her hair *always* perfectly set. Her lips *always* painted into a pretty red bow with such precision that Elizabeth Arden couldn't have done them better herself. Victory Red her favourite shade.

We headed into the dining room, where my husband was waiting. 'You're getting fatty,' she teased him, poking a manicured finger into his belly, 'but look at me, still bewdiful!' The diamanté clip in her hair shimmered as she turned her head to be admired.

My husband and I often joked that Nanna's hearing might go or her eyesight fade, but vanity would be the last thing to leave her before she died.

It really wasn't vanity, though; it was dignity, the rawest essence of humanity, which she held on to with all her being. It was her way of saying to the world, 'You've taken everything, but you will never take my pride.'

It was many years after I'd joined the Horowitz family that I began to learn Mindla's story. My husband, Ralph, would mimic Nanna swearing in Yiddish – which her pet parrot did too, much to our amusement – or relay a joke that his late Pop told when they were children.

Then one day he said to me, 'I've told you their story, right?'

Wrong.

He shared a skeleton version, recalling how Pop would tell his adored grandsons bedtime tales of grand circuses and colourful clowns. And of how the Nazis tried to kill them all.

He described rescuing his beautiful bride who was locked up in a Russian prison, and how they journeyed halfway around the world to eventually live happily ever after. But these were no fairy tales.

The journalist in me fired off a million questions as I was desperate to know the whole story, but sadly by then Pop was long gone, and the family consensus was that 'Nanna never talks about it so we don't ask in case it upsets her.' Fair enough. I certainly didn't want her to relive any of the awful things I'd heard.

As Mindla got older, though, and it was clear that our time with her was running out, my sense of desperation grew. It was important for our family, for my husband and our children to know who they were and where they came from, to understand what their grandparents and indeed great-grandparents endured, and how on earth they had escaped the Germans and made it to Australia.

At the risk of upsetting Nanna, conversations needed to be had.

When we visited the nursing home, we knew not to bring Nanna cakes or sweet treats because she wanted to 'keep her figure', but she loved cosmetics, especially the brightest of bright nail polish, and she *loved* to chat while painting her nails.

So one chilly autumn morning I armed myself with a supply of the fanciest new nail polish I could find, some notepads, a voice recorder and a rusty old tin of black-and-white photographs she'd given her daughter-in-law Meg (my mother-in-law), to look after. And, inspired by Mitch Albom's *Tuesdays with Morrie*, my very own Mondays with Mindla began.

One by one we'd go through the tatty images together.

'Nanna, who is this?' I'd ask, 'and where was this picture taken?' Always treading gently so as not to upset her.

'Vhy do you vant to know?' she'd say in her thick Polish accent, expertly sweeping the magenta varnish across a nail.

At first, she was more interested in talking about how her beloved 'Collingvood' was travelling on the AFL ladder and what her great-grandchildren were up to, but slowly I'd draw the conversation back to her and begin to peel away the layers of her life.

And so it went on, week after week, month after month. Each visit followed the same pattern.

After the nails were set, we'd head to the dining room for lunch, deftly avoiding the conga line of Zimmer frames.

At her table, we were always joined by four or five elderly women – Mindla liked an audience – and once my notepad appeared, we'd go through a familiar routine.

'Vhy do you vant to know?' she'd ask again. 'My story is nothing special.'

'Vat about her, and her, and her?' she asked, pointing a sparkling fingertip towards each of the dear, weathered faces before me. 'We are all the same.'

And then one day it clicked. Although the past was undoubtedly painful, Mindla wasn't necessarily re-traumatised by telling it; she just didn't think her story was anything out of the ordinary because so many of the people around her had an equally horrific story of escaping the Nazis. Of losing loved ones, of family they never saw again. Of lice-ridden bodies, of starvation. Of the stench of war and death. So much death. So much sadness.

Many of these precious elderly men and women with whom Nanna shared her final years had miraculously survived, beating Hitler at his evil game.

Despite her age and declining physical health, Mindla's mind remained razor sharp to the very end, and during the many hours we spent together she recalled her life to me in surprising detail. However, when she died in 2015 at the age of ninety-six, many words remained unspoken and questions unanswered. So I embarked on a years-long quest to piece together the jigsaw puzzle of her and Pop Horowitz's lives.

Many documents and records of life's most precious moments – births, deaths and marriages alike – have been lost, bombed or burnt into oblivion, and I am therefore incredibly grateful to the genealogists, historians, academics and volunteers who have generously given their time and expertise to assist me during this process, particularly Krystyna Duszniak, whose inimitable knowledge and connections helped uncover material that not only confirmed Mindla's memories, but also helped us find a lost family.

As I did not have the luxury of interviewing Pop, who passed away in 1989, I've relied on my interviews with Mindla and other family members, especially the grandchildren he adored, to recreate his story; plus photographs and interviews with his former television colleagues on GTV-9's *Tarax Show* in Australia. Among these people, I am notably grateful to the wonderful Ron Blaskett, who shared many memories of Pop before he passed away in 2018. Vale, Ron.

Some dialogue is based on the recollections of others.

Pop Horowitz, officially Moszjes Baruch Horowitz, was known by several other names at various stages of his life: Moses, Kubush the Clown, Kubus Armondo, Sloppo the Clown, Zaydee and Kubush. For ease of reading and continuity I have referred to him as Kubush, which was Nanna's name for him, throughout the book.

I hope you will read this story in the spirit in which it is intended. This is not a historical text and does not profess to be an academic document of the Holocaust; it is simply one woman's story, one family's account, told through their eyes. All attempts have been made to verify information as much as possible.

Hitler did his best to erase the existence, history and spirit of an entire people. Six million Jewish men, women and children were killed by the Nazi regime in World War II. It is impossible to comprehend.

Ultimately, Hitler failed. Why? Because these people have not been forgotten. Piece by piece, snippet by snippet, story by story, year after year the lives of Holocaust victims and survivors and their place in society are being lovingly restored and remembered, the fabric of their lives stitched back into place, acknowledged, understood and valued.

Those souls may have been lost, but they are still loved, still treasured, still talked about. We will honour their past, and their stories fuel our future.

We will never forget.

PART I

Before the War

PART 1

Before the War

CHAPTER ONE

Warsaw, Winter 1936

Mindla peels off a glove and rummages through her purse as she walks along Stawki Street.

Her fingers, nicked and numb from hours working the erratic sewing machines, fumble clumsily around the bottom of her bag, trying to find her key.

She turns the corner for home but, distracted, doesn't see the edge of the loose cobblestone as it catches the heel of her shoe and tips her heavily into the gutter. Her petite frame crumples in a heap and she sits dazed for a few moments until she begins to compose herself. Tears come, but the icy wind whipping straight up from the Vistula steals them before she has time to wipe them away.

'Damn,' she says, fingering a hole in her threadbare woollen stockings, already repaired so many times that they are more darn than hose.

Her ankle throbs.

She can see her building, number 17 Muranowska Street,

right across the square. Her landlord, Mr Landau, will be tucked up warm and cosy in his first-floor apartment. In that moment she longs for home and the warmth of her mother's kitchen. She imagines Mama at the table flouring and rolling challah dough, and the smell of coal scraps burning as the stove heats up to just the right temperature for the bread to rise.

Lost in her thoughts, she doesn't see the stranger appear.

'What are you doing out here? It is not safe,' the voice says, startling her back into reality. 'Are you okay?'

Her head has to tilt right back to catch the face of a tall man standing over her, his arm outstretched.

Mindla takes his hand and he gently helps her up off the freezing stone. 'Let me escort you home,' he insists. He pulls off his scarf and offers it to her.

She gladly wraps the soft warm wool around her neck and they chat about the arrival of winter as she hobbles across the tram tracks. He asks where she works. Mindla hesitates, before saying simply, 'The tannery.' She doesn't mention that she has had to work there since she was old enough to leave school at the age of fourteen, or how hard the dirty, smelly work is: the long hours of curing and stretching animal skins, staining and dyeing them. The tannery is the main supplier of saddlery and leather goods to the Polish army. With the constant threat of war, business is booming.

The more she walks the more the ankle settles and with each step she feels her strength return.

The soft light from Mr Landau's apartment allows a proper glimpse of the stranger's face. He is surprisingly young for someone so well dressed, possibly in his mid-twenties. A red silk kerchief pokes out of his top pocket. His suit gives the impression of a much older businessman, but his big blue eyes sparkle like a mischievous child's.

'My name is Kubush Horowitz,' he says as they reach the doorway. 'And you are?'

'Mindla. Mindla Levin,' she says, bowing her head.

'So, Miss Levin, you are home safe.'

'Thank you, Kubush. You are very kind.'

She hands back his scarf and with that he tips his hat and walks away. Gone almost as quickly as he arrived.

'You're late, Mindla,' Chana says, raising an eyebrow. 'Hurry up and sit down.'

'Sorry, Mama,' Mindla replies, tugging her dress over the hole in her hose.

All eyes turn to the teenager as she clumsily squeezes in between her sisters Jadzia and Sonia to take her place at the table. She keeps her head down to avoid her father's stare, her stained fingers tracing invisible rings around the dark wood knots poking through her mother's thinning white tablecloth.

She is seated on the long wooden bench along one side of the table and can almost hear the old pine slab groaning under the weight of them all. Since her sister Eva's husband,

Laloshe, moved in, eleven now jostle for elbow room around Chana Levin's kitchen table.

Mindla's eyes follow her mother as she passes the baby on her hip to Eva.

Her hair, greying prematurely, is swept back in a neat bun, allowing the candlelight to fully illuminate her face. Not for the first time Mindla notices the sickly dark circles under her mother's eyes and silently vows never to be late for dinner again.

CHAPTER TWO

Darkness chases Mindla along the cobblestones of Muranowska Street as she hurries home from the factory again, this time watching for every errant step.

'There is a letter for you, Mindla,' Mr Landau says as she bursts through the street door. Mr Landau employs many of the tenants at his leather factory and is a kind man who regularly forgives late payment of the rent when money is tight. 'Hand-delivered . . .' He grins.

She assumes he means it is a letter for her father because she never receives mail, but her name etched in the most beautiful cursive handwriting instantly catches her eye, stopping her in her tracks. Fingers stained brown from a day at the tannery fumble in her haste to prise open the creamy velvet envelope.

Dear Miss Levin,

I hope your ankle is improving. Would you be my guest for a performance of the Circus Staniewski tomorrow evening?

If so, I will meet you at 7 pm. If you are not on the street where we first met, I will assume you do not wish to join me.

Sincerely,

Mr Kubush Horowitz

The handsome stranger.

She carefully tucks the precious letter back inside the envelope and holds it close to her pounding heart as she runs up the noisy wooden stairs.

'Thank you, Mr Landau,' Mindla sings out, skipping every second step.

'Again, Mindla?' Chana says impatiently. Two candles illuminate the feast her mother has spent the day preparing and the delicious smell of her challah, straight from the oven, butters the guilt of Mindla's late arrival. She catches the scent of the fresh rosemary decorating the table as she takes her place. Chana extends her hands forward and waves them over the candles. Then she covers her eyes as her honey voice hums the familiar Kiddush prayer: *'Vah'hi erev vay'hi boker yom hashishi.'*

Shabbas has begun.

Shmuel and Chana Levin aren't particularly religious people but tradition is important, and despite thinning cupboards Chana always manages to fill the Shabbas table. She is a homemaker and Mindla only ever knows her mother pregnant or with a baby on her hip. First it was Eva in 1916, followed closely by Jadzia, then Mindla a year or so later in 1919. With Sonia's arrival in 1921 Chana had four daughters under the age of five. Shmuel's longing for a son was fulfilled when Yakov arrived in 1922, and then good fortune blessed them again with Menachem and Minya. And finally, at least they all hoped, baby Shara.

Mindla feels guilty that there isn't a minute of her mother's day not taken up with cooking, cleaning, washing and caring for others, a pot on the stove and nappies soaking in a galvanised iron bucket beneath the sink. She loves watching her mother work, though; she is a maestro in the kitchen, conducting an unruly and often pitiful orchestra. When Chana is in full flight, she can make every corner of the kitchen sing. The crackle of the coal-fired oven, pots on the stove, the rhythmic thud of dough being rolled and kneaded into shape on the bench; and once a week she somehow manages to bring it all together in a delicious Shabbas crescendo.

Mindla especially loves Jewish New Year when Chana invites all of the girls into her kitchen to help make kichel biscuits, which melt in their mouths as quickly as their fingers snatch them from the oven.

Chana's kitchen table provides more than food, it is also a pine slab pulpit from where she delivers life sermons, her wisdom and traditions, stories and home-grown lessons all kneaded together and adding to the richness of her soups and challah.

Tonight Chana's table is a place of worship. Mindla glances at her father, who is watching her mother admiringly as she recites the blessings. Shmuel is a cobbler who works hard to make ends meet. With a little spit and polish, and the offcuts of leather from Mr Landau's factory, he can make an old pair of shoes look new again. Neighbours describe him as 'an artiste' and he is terribly good at his craft. They'll bring him shoes that are long past wearable, but Shmuel works his magic on them day and night, delivering them back to their grateful owners with a new lease of life. Repairing old shoes doesn't pay well, however; certainly not enough to make life comfortable for the growing mouths the Levins have to feed. Shmuel's clients are also very poor and he often refuses payment for his work, knowing that the shoes would have been the only pair a desperate man had for getting to work and to market to feed his family. How can he charge such a man? Sometimes he'll be paid with a loaf of bread or an egg or two, on a very good day some butter or a chicken. Mindla is proud of her father and never complains that her wages often go straight back to Mr Landau to help pay the rent.

As her mother removes her hands from her eyes and looks at the candles to complete the ritual, Mindla wonders how many other families are doing the same thing in the building. One hundred and ten families live at 17 Muranowska Street at the northern tip of Warsaw's Jewish quarter. Four- or five-storey buildings face one another around a square that is used for gatherings, markets and entertainment. Tramcars and rickshaws ferry people through its heart. Many of the residents are big families like the Levins, and Mindla guesses there must be seven or eight hundred people living above and below them.

Jadzia's impending marriage will add one more face to their Shabbas table, but unlike Eva and Laloshe who live at Muranowska Street, Jadzia plans to move into her fiancé Avraham Ksiazenicer's apartment after their wedding. Thank goodness.

As the girls settle into bed later that evening, Mindla confides in Jadzia and Eva about the handsome stranger who rescued her, and his invitation. Their eyes widen at the letter she pulls out from under her pillow.

'I have never seen such beautiful paper,' Jadzia says, thumbing the thick card.

As with all of the girls in the Levin family, Mindla's marriage will be arranged by her father, at a time and to a groom of his choosing. The idea of his daughter meeting a stranger, let alone going on a date to the circus with him, is unthinkable.

'You must go, Mindla!' Jadzia whispers, squeezing her sister's hand excitedly, 'Just think – the circus! What a treat. We'll help.'

Mindla can barely sleep that night, and over breakfast the following morning, she and her sisters hatch their plan.

'Mama, I think it would be nice if Mindla came to dinner with Laloshe and me this evening,' Eva says very casually as her mother busies herself in the kitchen. 'It's his father's birthday and the Rabbi is coming.'

11

'It would be good for her to be around more grown up company,' Jadzia adds, nodding to the grubby little faces of her three youngest siblings lined up at the table waiting for their porridge.

Chana places bowls on the table, face unreadable. Finally she nods. 'But don't bring her home too late,' she warns.

As the last rays of light retreat that Saturday evening, the family gathers back around the table and Shmuel makes Havdalah to mark the end of Shabbas. He lifts a cup of wine and shares a blessing with those before him, then draws his fingers towards the candle flame, allowing the light to illuminate his skin. He signals for them all to follow. As a child Mindla loved this special ceremony but now when she holds her hands up to the candles, they glow orange and she is embarrassed.

Mindla keeps one eye on the clock and one eye on Papa. She is itching to get out the door and worried that if she is not there when Kubush arrives, he may not wait.

Eva and Jadzia are just as excited as Mindla. Eva insisted Mindla wear the beautiful navy silk dress Chana made for her engagement, while Jadzia scooped Mindla's hair off her face and pinned her long chestnut rolls back carefully so her curls rested gently on her shoulders. Mindla painted her lips into a perfect bow, deliciously carmine red.

Now she is tingling with excitement and each minute feels like an eternity.

With a sip of the blessed wine, Shmuel declares Shabbas over and the girls are free to leave. They are careful not to arouse suspicion, calmly saying goodnight to everyone, even though they are out the door barely a minute later.

Eva snakes an arm through Mindla's and they casually wander down the street, past the building and away from prying eyes to meet Kubush, who is rounding the corner of the street.

Kubush Horowitz is even more handsome than Mindla remembers. The azure polka-dot kerchief poking out of his suit pocket brings out the blue in his eyes. The woollen scarf he'd wrapped around her two nights earlier is around his neck.

'Eva, this is Kubush,' Mindla says, introducing them.

Eva smiles and shakes Kubush's hand. He tips his hat to her.

'Meet me in front of the coffee shop at 10 pm,' Eva instructs her little sister, 'and don't be a minute late, Mindla, or you're on your own.'

CHAPTER THREE

The air is crisp and the snow is almost nipping at Mindla's heels as they hurry through the backstreets of Warsaw towards the circus. The temperature is dropping and any day now the city will be blanketed in white.

It is a good twenty-minute walk to the corner of Ordynacka and Okolnik streets where the gold-leafed auditorium of the Cyrk Staniewski stretches around the block. The building lay dormant for many years until it was purchased by the local Staniewski brothers in 1929. Bronislaw and Mieczyslaw Staniewski poured heart and soul and a good deal of money into reviving the building to its former glory, and they quickly earned a reputation for their elaborate and often avant-garde performances. Each season the brothers unveiled an ambitious new show, bringing guests from overseas and daring themselves to be bigger and brighter.

'It is not easy to meet the demands of the fastidious Warsaw audiences,' Bronislaw told journalists at the opening of the 1936 season, 'but this time I can say that I can sleep peacefully at night. This program has no equal in the history of our circus.'

As Kubush leads Mindla around the corner from Okolnik Street into Ordynacka they step around horse-drawn carts as the striking domed roof comes into full view. Up close it is even more breathtaking than she'd imagined. Other than some elaborate churches and the great synagogue, she has never seen such a lavish display of wealth before.

People are milling around the marble steps of the entrance, waiting in line for the box office, but rather than joining the queue, Kubush places his hand on her elbow and gently guides her through the crowd and straight into the foyer. 'Witaj, Kubush' – *Good evening, Kubush* – the doorman says, greeting him with warm familiarity, as the usher arrives to show them to their seats. She wonders how he is known here and her mind races with possibilities, but she does not feel she can ask.

The front row circling the main arena is already full. Women wrapped in beautiful furs and men in smart felt fedoras are cosied up in velvet-lined booths reserved for VIP guests. Mindla and Kubush are shown to their seats, just a few rows behind.

As she slips into the soft leather, Mindla's senses begin to register the spectacle around her. She's never been to a theatre performance, let alone the circus. Women in silk dresses and silver fox hats spill out of the dress circle above. Enormous crystal chandeliers drip from the exquisite domed roof. She counts eight of them before the thinnest of wires, weaving between the chandeliers – she assumes in readiness for the highwire walkers – catches her eye.

A clap from the cymbals of the orchestra warming up their instruments brings Mindla back to earth and suddenly she becomes aware of the sweet smell of sawdust drifting up from the arena. 'Thank you, Kubush,' she whispers.

'The show hasn't even begun!' he replies, smiling.

Soon, the chandeliers dim and a spotlight from somewhere high above shines down on the arena. Drums roll into a thundering crescendo as a riderless white horse bursts through velvet curtains then stops centre stage and takes a bow.

The graceful stallion proudly gallops a lap of the arena in time to the music, and as the tempo changes, he too changes pace and dances in time to the different drumbeat.

A pretty woman in a flowing white gown follows the horse into the spotlight and guides him through his performance.

After his first lap, the horse comes to attention beside her, then mimics her as she bows her head to the audience. 'Bravo!' the audience cries, as the proud steed places one leg forward and bends his head in a mock curtsey.

'So clever!' Mindla says, shaking her head in disbelief as the crowd erupts again and the horse canters offstage.

Just as they think the act is over, the white horse gallops back through the curtain once again, this time with a cheeky little chimpanzee jockeying on his back. The monkey is dressed up in a suit and pants, a checked vest and matching bow tie, with a grin from ear to ear. As they pass the pretty ringmaster, the chimp leaps from the horse's back straight into the woman's arms, while the horse races out of the arena. A perfect dismount.

Mindla's hands ache from clapping and the circus is only just warming up! It is 'The Princess Abyssinia Koringa' who this packed house has come to see and the audience roars with delight as she glides seductively into the limelight.

The beautiful contortionist bows, then begins slowly twisting her limbs into all manner of painful-looking positions. She arches backwards so far that her seemingly rubber body is folded in half, then pokes her head between her legs, waving as a slow drum roll heralds the arrival of a coffin into the arena. The human corkscrew unwinds herself and eases into the coffin, which is sealed and locked before the audience's wide eyes.

An audible gasp sweeps the theatre as she is lowered into a shallow grave dug into the arena. Clowns shovel sand on top of her. Time ticks by impossibly slowly while this woman is buried alive and unable to breathe, and the tension builds with the timpani's rolling beat.

After what feels like an eternity, a delicate hand finally appears through the sand. The crowd roars with delight and the clowns race to the 'grave' to lift her free. After she takes a triumphant bow the coffin is raised to reveal the locks are still in place and the coffin fully sealed.

But how did she escape? Mindla is dumbfounded. Oh, the secrets of a grand circus!

Jugglers and clowns race around the arena, entertaining the crowd in between the star acts. The audience cracks up with laughter when one of them steals the expensive watch from a wealthy but unsuspecting guest in the front row.

'So cheeky!' Mindla enthuses.

The next act is a towering man accompanied by a young child, introduced as 'Beetz and son'. Beetz is carrying a bamboo pole, about six metres long. He positions himself in the centre of the spotlight, kneeling with the bamboo staked beside him. The boy, who looks about ten or eleven, steps onto his father's knee, and then, using the bamboo for support, climbs onto his shoulders. Once he is stable, Beetz carefully stands and slides the bamboo up higher, resting it on top of his thigh. The boy shimmies right to the top and every muscle of Beetz's sinewy body begins to tense. He steadies the pole while the child folds his legs underneath himself and forms a sitting position, balanced on the tip of the bamboo. One false move from Beetz and the boy will come tumbling down.

The audience breaks into applause. 'Marvellous! Marvellous!' they cheer.

For the next few minutes the child manoeuvres his little body into an upright handstand on the tippy top of the pole. But far from it being the end of the act, he then slowly stretches one arm out until he balances solely on one hand.

'One arm! Impossible!' a woman shouts from behind Mindla. 'I cannot look!'

Mindla feels the same way.

Releasing the handstand, the child swings his legs back onto the pole, wrapping them around the bamboo before sliding down to the second perfect dismount of the evening so far. The audience, which has been holding its breath while watching the little boy, heaves a collective sigh. For the next two hours Mindla's heart leaps with every twist and turn.

Trapeze artists fly through the sky, trampolinists fall to earth into tiny nets from the very top of the domed roof, and a colourful cast of animals — lions and tigers, dancing dogs and a petulant pig — take Mindla's breath away. And just when she thinks the show is over, the little monkey comes bursting through the curtains riding a bicycle, chased by a fumbling clown.

She claps until her fingers burn.

'Bravo, bravo,' voices around her cheer. 'Encore!'

As the audience trickles out of the arena, Kubush reaches for Mindla's arm. 'We'll go this way,' he says, forging a path through the crush of people. 'I'd like you to meet some friends.'

Curious about where this next adventure may take them, she follows him. They weave between rows of empty seats down to the arena, whereupon Kubush tugs open the heavy red velvet curtains and ushers Mindla through. The back-stage area is bustling with activity and she struggles to take it all in. Horses are being fed, acrobats are stretching their weary muscles and the clowns are crowding around little mirrors, beginning to unmask.

It is a magical mayhem of animals and performers.

Kubush shakes hands with almost everyone they come across as he leads her through makeshift dressing rooms.

'Good evening, Pawel,' he says to the man Mindla recognises as the trainer of the dancing dogs. 'Good show!'

She follows him along a passageway filled with racks of sparkling costumes, past a door marked with 'Princess Abyssinia' below a big gold star, and onwards to another dressing room. He knocks politely and a woman's voice beckons him in.

'Kubush!' she says with delight, kissing him on both cheeks, 'so good to see you!'

Mindla instantly recognises her as the dressage ringmaster whose glorious white horse danced with such precision at the beginning of the show. Up close, she is older than Mindla realised but even more beautiful than the glamorous figure they'd watched under the arena's spotlight. A short dark bob pokes out from under her sleek black velvet hat, her creamy skin radiant without the heavy stage make-up. 'Did you enjoy the show?' she asks.

'More than ever!' he assures her, before adding with a wink, 'but as usual the clowns were the highlight.'

'Mindla, I'd like you to meet Mrs Lala Staniewska. Lala's husband, Bronislaw, is the ringmaster of the circus, but everyone knows who the real boss of this grand *chapiteau* is,' he says, giving her a cheeky nod.

Lala smiles indulgently.

'Lala, this is Mindla's first time to the circus.'

'How wonderful, Mindla, what did you think?' she asks.

'It is the most magical thing I've ever seen,' Mindla gushes, 'my hands are still sore from clapping!'

'Well, thank you, that's what we like to hear. And I'm assuming we will be seeing you next week?' Lala asks Kubush.

'Monday, 6 am on the dot.'

'Excellent. I must away to join my husband. He is supposed to be entertaining some reporters who came to review the show. I will see you on Monday, Kubush. Lovely to meet you, Mindla.'

As Kubush and Mindla hurry through the backstreets of Warsaw in time for their rendezvous with Eva, Kubush Horowitz reveals that he is also known as Kubush the Clown, a performer of the Circus Staniewski touring troupe that travels all around Poland performing under a big-top tent. In winter, the touring circus goes into recess, but next week they begin their rehearsals and preparations for new acts and a new show to take out to the Polish countryside in spring.

Mindla finds it hard to imagine this debonair man in his crisp wool suit and hat playing tomfoolery in glad rags. She longs to know more about him and is disappointed when, before she knows it, she finds herself outside the coffee shop.

As promised, Eva is waiting.

'Thank you, Kubush, I will never forget this night,' she says, reluctantly saying goodbye.

'Perhaps you will join me for a walk sometime?' he asks.

'Oh, I'd enjoy that very much.'

'Well?' Eva whispers, grabbing her sister's hands as they watch Kubush walk away. 'Tell me everything!'

Where can Mindla even begin? The horses, the tigers, the trapeze, the monkey, the Princess Abyssinia, the colour and excitement! Over the short distance back to their apartment, words tumble out. She knows she is hardly making any sense but as they reach the steps of 17 Muranowska Street, Mindla pauses and squeezes her sister's hand tight.

'Eva, it was the most wonderful night of my life.'

Eva smiles. 'My lips are sealed.'

CHAPTER FOUR

Kubush Horowitz is a man of his word. A few days later there is another letter waiting with Mr Landau. Mindla recognises the beautiful cream envelope immediately and opens it as fast as her fingers allow. As promised, it is an invitation to go for a walk during the coming weekend.

Heading back upstairs she feels as if she is floating on air, tingling with the excitement of this forbidden romance.

What would her father do if he found out? A knot rises in her stomach that she does her best to ignore. For a few precious moments, she doesn't care to think.

Jadzia and Eva help. Kubush meets the girls at the end of Muranowska and he and Mindla lose themselves in the bustle of Nowolipki and Leszno streets. Eva and Jadzia discreetly walk ahead, keeping a keen eye on who is around them, stopping every now and then to admire the fancy wares in Mr Puterman's window or the delicious golden kippers

Mr Hen has lined up in wooden boxes outside his store, giving the young couple precious moments to talk. At first their conversations are about Mindla and her family, but gradually Kubush reveals a little more about himself. About how he came from Lwow to the south-east of Warsaw, close to the Russian border. How his family were poor and his mother, Golda, spent most of her life pregnant. 'She died when I was fourteen,' he told her, turning away from Mindla so she couldn't see his face, 'and my father remarried soon afterwards because he needed someone to help raise his eight children.'

Mindla knows not to pry; that he will tell her more when he's ready.

Over the next few weeks Mindla and Kubush snatch precious moments together, mindful of the risk that if Shmuel finds out, Mindla will never be allowed to see Kubush again.

They continue to find ways to see each other. Sometimes it's a clandestine coffee, sometimes a fleeting glance at Shul; regardless, Mindla thinks about Kubush night and day. Time stands still when she is with him and the thought of seeing him, even for the briefest moment, makes the long, hard days at the tannery bearable. One day they are together when a soldier in uniform passes by.

'I almost joined the army,' Kubush confesses. 'I didn't see eye to eye with my stepmother and by my fifteenth birthday I'd decided to sign up with my brothers, Albert and Jakub. Until the circus came to town that is.'

He begins to tell the story of how the Cyrk Staniewski rolled into Lwow with great fanfare in the summer of 1925. The circus was still in its infancy but the touring big top had earned a reputation throughout the Polish countryside. The circus had travelled down the eastern border, from Bialystok to Lublin, Chelm and Lwow and was circling back to the west, pitching the big top in Krosno and Krakow. The last stop would be Warsaw for the winter recess.

When word spread that the painted wooden caravans were on the horizon, Kubush and his brothers raced to the outskirts of town to greet them. With a bird's-eye view from the top of a towering horse chestnut tree, they watched as the big top began to take shape and handlers released animals from their cages to stretch their legs.

'Don't just sit up there,' a voice called, 'come down and make yourselves useful.'

With that invitation, the Horowitz brothers scurried down from their perch and put themselves to work.

The circus foreman enlisted the three strapping young men to form a human anchor at the bottom of a thick guide rope that hoisted an enormous wooden pole into place to hold up the tent.

It was thirsty work and the knotted rope burnt their palms as it slipped through their fingers and resisted their grip, but it sure beat ploughing fields and picking turnips. When the pole was upright, they were each given a mallet and took turns hammering long steel pegs into the earth to secure the pole's guide ropes. When the first one was successfully raised, they then started on poles two, three and four, which would support the enormous black canvas tent stretched out behind them. Finally, when the poles were stabilised and the shiny canvas raised from the earth, forming the circus tent, the Horowitz boys were given the task of shovelling piles of sand into the centre to form the base of the main arena.

Once the sand was in place, it had to be compacted with a metal roller and then sawdust layered on top. 'You boys have done a good job today,' the foreman said, handing each of them a prized ticket to come along to the show. At 4 pm the following day, dressed in their finest pants, handed down from brother to brother, and clean white shirts borrowed from their father and a neighbour, Kubush, Albert and Jakub Horowitz went off to the circus.

By any standards this was a spectacle. It seemed like the whole of Lwow was crammed in under the big top.

The most expensive seats at the edge of the arena were sold out; at seven zloty each this was more than a week's wage for the average farm worker. The brothers squeezed themselves among men and women, jostling for position along the wooden bleachers that lined the back of the tent.

For the next two hours, they hardly took a breath, soaking in the sights and sounds of the Cyrk Staniewski. They clapped, cheered and finger-whistled when the Chinese juggler Chin-Chan-Cho tossed one ball, then two, three, four, five, six and seven into the air, catching and releasing them again at lightning speed.

They laughed until their stomachs hurt when a little monkey, dressed in a suit, ran out onto the arena and climbed up into the lap of a well-known politician sitting in the front row. After cosying himself on the man's lap, the monkey lit up a cigar and smoked it! The laughter almost lifted the tent right off its steel pegs. But the star performer they'd all been waiting to see was the strongman Zygmunt Breitbart, who could pull apart thick steel chains with his teeth. Many thought his act was trickery, so to prove the doubters wrong the ringmaster invited the audience to bring along their own chains to test him. His superhuman strength left many a challenger red-faced.

For one carefree night, the people of Lwow, rich and poor alike, forgot about their struggles and indulged in the magic the Staniewski brothers delivered. Crazy clowns, somersaulting acrobats and exotic women dripping in sequins and feathers were a feast for any young man's eyes. That night Kubush barely slept and at dawn he raced back to the circus again to see if they needed help. He was prepared to do any job that was going if it meant another free ticket.

As luck would have it, Bronislaw Staniewski needed someone to help feed the animals and muck out their pens. His regular man was stricken with typhus and had had to be quarantined from the camp; he wouldn't be back to work any time soon. For the next two weeks while the circus was in Lwow, Kubush showed up every morning at dawn to help feed the animals and shovel away their muck.

With a large number of pens to be cleaned it was hard work, but he loved every minute. He particularly enjoyed the few seconds he'd get close to the tigers. Cleaning out their caravan was a fine art. When the handler was ready, he would chain up the five big cats and unbolt the gates to their cage. The tigers would launch out of the cage, often with the handler running after them, giving Kubush just a few minutes to clean the wooden pen of stale straw and tiger manure, then add fresh straw and be back out by the time they returned. On his last day, Kubush was rewarded with a ticket to attend the circus's final show, but by then he'd set himself a new goal. After he finished his work, Kubush politely knocked on the door of Bronislaw Staniewski's caravan.

'Good morning, sir,' he said, sheepishly tipping his hat to the towering man who was wearing a black top-hat and dashing gold and red ringmaster's costume.

'Ah, Kubush, good boy. I'll get your ticket; thank you for your help.'

'It was a pleasure, sir. Sir, I was wondering if there was any chance of continuing on with the circus to the next town?' he asked.

Kubush's ability to keep out of the way and not annoy anyone must have impressed Bronislaw Staniewski. With his regular muck man still stricken with illness and unlikely to return, he didn't hesitate in his response.

'We decamp tonight immediately after the show. Be ready.'

The young scallywag ran all the way home, dodging and weaving through tramcars and horses along Sloneczna

Street, his smile wider than the entrance of Gimpel's Yiddish Theatre. By the time he reached the old market he was almost dancing down the cobblestones, snatching an apple from a stand on his way through.

'May the flies stick to you,' the vendor cried out as Kubush flashed a cheeky smile and darted through the crowd.

He could barely catch his breath as he burst through the front door and ran upstairs to their apartment.

'Papa,' he yelled. 'I've got a job with the circus; I'm leaving tonight.'

Mendel Horowitz watched on in both confusion and bewilderment as his son stuffed his meagre belongings into an old hessian sack.

Once the makeshift duffel bag was full, he tied the corners and took a deep breath.

'Opshtel, opshtel!' – *Stop!* Mendel chided him and demanded he sit for a few minutes over tea to explain this folly.

'But what about the army?' Mendel asked, confused by the excitement of the young man.

'I'll be back, Papa. I promise,' he said in between mouthfuls of the boiled egg his father pushed across the kitchen table towards him. 'I promise, Papa, after the next town I'll be home.'

He kissed the old man's balding head and collected his single bag on his way out the door.

'Goodbye, Papa,' he called.

•

One afternoon Kubush invites Jadzia and Mindla to visit the stables at the back of Ordynacka Street where the Staniewskis keep their horses. Mindla discovers that the white stallion who captured her heart at the circus loves to be tickled under his chin and be fed. Jadzia offers him a handful of chaff and he cheekily nudges her again and again for more.

'Oh, you greedy boy!' she giggles, stroking his long white mane as he nuzzles into her.

Small stalls sit off the main cobblestone path, home to a menagerie of little ponies, handsome stallions, and a pig. Mindla reaches through the wooden posts to offer the swine a wilted potato from the slops bucket at the gate, but the brazen animal snatches it from her hand and gobbles it down before she can blink.

The pig seems very pleased with himself and stands to attention, hopeful of more. Mindla bursts out laughing. She can feel Kubush's eyes on her and blushes.

'You really are the most beautiful girl I've ever seen, Mindla Levin,' he says.

Her heart leaps and she skips all the way home with Jadzia trailing behind pleading, 'Mindla, you *must* talk to Mama and Papa. We cannot continue to help you like this. If Papa finds out you will never be able to see Kubush again, and he will never forgive us.'

She is right, but Mindla needs to choose the moment carefully.

•

The snows Warsaw has endured for most of February are beginning to turn to slush underfoot and the weak rays of sunlight are strengthening a little each day.

Buds of cherry blossom dot the trees and the stems of crocuses push through the chilled soil, their purple flowers soon to brighten up the city's gardens. The arrival of spring is bittersweet for Mindla; she is excited that Jadzia will soon be married but knows it will shortly be time for Kubush to move on. The Staniewskis' country caravan is almost ready for the summer touring season. Rehearsals are well underway, new acts have been brought in to the show and the program almost set. By April they'll be on the road.

Jadzia is in the kitchen sewing with Chana when Mindla finally plucks up the courage to blurt out, 'Mama, I have met someone very nice and I would like you and Papa to meet him.'

'Him?' Chana says, pausing mid-stitch to look up. 'Who is this *him* and where did you meet? At the factory?'

'No,' Mindla says, explaining how Kubush helped when she fell over. She goes on to carefully reveal that Kubush is a clown with a wonderful circus and how he has invited her to go and watch him perform, wisely editing recent history. 'He sounds like a gentleman,' Jadzia offers cautiously, keeping tight-lipped about her role in this courtship.

'A clown does not make a husband, Mindla,' Chana says. 'What life is this, sleeping in tents? Your father will choose someone of our kind.'

Mindla reasons that Kubush is indeed 'of our kind', a Jewish man from a poor family who is working hard, a man so funny and clever he can make anyone laugh, hopefully even Papa.

'Please, Mama, will you speak to Papa?'

'He sounds very nice,' Jadzia adds. 'It won't hurt if Papa meets him.'

Chana keeps her eyes focused on her mending. Reluctantly she nods.

Ten days later, after some convincing, one more person sits around the Shabbas table.

Chana Levin is delighted with the bag of shiny red apples that Kubush brings for her; he certainly knows how to charm.

Shmuel Levin, however, is harder to impress, especially when Kubush talks about circus life. 'From town to town, never in the same bed,' Shmuel says, grimacing. He does not say aloud that he thinks they are glorified gypsies.

'Maybe you will come one day, Mr Levin?' he asks.

'A man has no need for a circus,' Shmuel replies staunchly.

After dinner Menachem barely waits a minute before asking Kubush to teach him how to juggle. Kubush agrees, patiently showing the nine-year-old again and again how to get started. 'Now, toss the ball into the air,' Kubush says. 'Now add another,' he says as the boy drops the balls to the ground.

'Okay, let's start again.'

After Kubush is gone, Shmuel echoes his wife's initial concerns.

'What does a man like this want with a poor Jewish girl?' he asks sceptically. Jadzia and Eva work their magic, convincing Papa that there are very few suitable young men for Mindla and if she misses this opportunity with Kubush she may never marry.

'I won't say you have my blessing, Mindla. This is not how these things are done, but I see you smiling,' Papa says. He adds, 'A clown is not a husband, Mindla. He will forget about you when he goes to the next town and you will be sorry, then no-one will marry you. Nothing good comes from a clown.'

With her father's qualified permission, Kubush and Mindla meet as often as they can. Then on a Sunday afternoon, as they feed the horses at the Staniewski stables, Kubush asks Mindla to marry him. Her father reluctantly agrees to give his blessing, even though he continues to mutter 'a clown is not a husband' under his breath.

On the eve of Kubush's farewell, they are married under a cream calico chuppah at the home of Chana's cousin. Shmuel and Chana can't afford another wedding so soon after Jadzia, but relatives offer to help. About thirty people come, just family. It is a simple ceremony minus many of the regular trimmings you would enjoy at a Jewish wedding, but the bride and groom don't care. They are deliriously happy.

Chana's family prepare all of the food and organise the Rabbi. Mindla is radiant, wearing the dress that Jadzia had worn at her own wedding only a few weeks earlier. After they make their vows, Shmuel hands Kubush a glass wrapped in a piece of linen.

Kubush stomps on the glass and breaks it, and from that moment on their souls are united, never to part. 'Mazel tov!' everyone cheers.

CHAPTER FIVE

Summer 1936

While Kubush is away touring it makes sense for Mindla to remain in Warsaw. During the day she continues working at Mr Landau's tannery, and at night she helps her mother with the younger children. Kubush sends money, which helps the family greatly.

Long before dawn one morning, Shmuel gently shakes his daughter awake.

'Mindla, Mama is sick, I need your help to prepare breakfast.'

Rubbing her eyes, Mindla quietly gets a pot of porridge going on the stove then makes Mama some tea. At first, she wonders if another baby is on the way, heaven forbid.

But her mother's trembling fingers can barely lift the cup to her lips, and the feverish sweat that glues her thin nightie to her wilted breasts is not the familiar sign she is carrying.

Eva wakes with the noise and gets into bed beside Mama,

35

holding cold compresses to her forehead. Mindla begs Papa to call the doctor, but he resists.

'She'll be fine,' he reassures her. 'She just needs some rest.'

Later in the morning when Menachem and Minya have gone to school, Shmuel fetches their neighbour Mrs Feigelblum from upstairs. He says Mrs Feigelblum's homemade lotions and potions are better than any medicine a doctor could prescribe. Mindla grimaces at the thought of the foul-tasting concoctions she pours down their throats when they are sick. She is certain they only feel better because the stinky syrup tastes so disgusting it takes their minds off the actual symptoms of being ill.

Shmuel helps Mama limp into the kitchen, where she sits by the warmth of the stove, wrapped in a blanket and shivering.

Mindla watches wide-eyed as Mrs Feigelblum unpacks a bag and gets down to work. She dips the end of a cotton-wrapped stick into a glass jar containing some sort of white spirit, then lights the stick with a flame from the stove.

Once the tip is alight, she places it inside a glass until the rim is smoking hot, then she quickly applies the burning glass to Mama's back. The suction sticks the glass to Mama's translucent skin. Mrs Feigelblum repeats this painful routine until Mama's back is covered in red welts. She calls it *banki* and says it draws the badness from your blood.

The last step in Mrs Feigelblum's treatment is a good swig of a brown-bottled brew, after which Mama shuffles back to bed and sleeps for the next two days.

Sure enough, the magic works and when Chana Levin

wakes, she is back to herself again. As Mrs Feigelblum promised, the badness has gone from her blood.

Mindla can't recall a specific moment when she becomes aware that the mood towards Jews has changed; it's more a gradual sense of unease.

Each evening Papa listens to a little crystal set Laloshe has made for him while he painstakingly stitches and polishes the last of the day's shoes. Through the crackling static, they learn of the problems unfolding across the border in Germany. One day it's the Nuremberg Laws, decreeing that only those of pure German blood are now eligible to be Reich citizens, rendering Jews in Germany second-class citizens. Another day, it's the burning of books by Jewish authors or the destruction of Jewish businesses.

Papa shakes his head in disbelief.

Sometimes he stays up well into the night after he finishes his work, unable to sleep and contemplating the worrying events abroad.

Over breakfast Papa shares what he learns and none of the news is good. Stories reach Poland of Jews being randomly rounded up or dragged from their homes, of Jewish doctors banned from practising medicine, Jewish teachers banned from teaching and even Jewish organists forbidden to play in churches. Such pointless hate.

Riots against Jews break out on the streets of Berlin, and German girls are warned to stay away from Jewish men or they will be committing a sin against the Führer. More and more villages celebrate being judenrein – cleansed of Jews – and thousands begin to flee to safety, some to the United States, some to France and Palestine and some to Poland.

Those who cross the border bring tales of persecution, a dark fear in their eyes.

Soon the news shared around Chana's table is from Poland, not from across the border. The seeds of hate have been sown in Germany but green shoots are quickly springing up around Poland.

'I hear that Jewish students at the university are being spat on,' Laloshe tells the family over dinner one evening. While the younger children continue slurping up their soup, oblivious to the meaning of this news, the adults react with a stunned silence.

Shmuel shakes his head in pent-up rage, nervously flipping his butter knife over.

'Segregation. This is segregation. What will become of us?' he exclaims.

Then death arrives in the village of Przytyk on the outskirts of Radom. Three people are killed and twenty-four injured when Polish farmers turn on local Jewish stallholders at the town market. Armed with sticks and stones they storm Jewish homes, smashing windows and breaking furniture. A Jewish cobbler and his wife are tortured to death. Their children, who were discovered cowering under their beds, are savagely beaten.

This news snatches Mindla's sleep. She worries about Kubush who is touring through the small towns and villages to the south of Warsaw, not far from where these attacks take place. She comforts herself that he never mentions such fear in any of his letters; he only shares news of sell-out shows and the hijinks of life on the road. Nevertheless, she counts down the days until he will be home safe in her arms.

On 1 August the Levins all gather around the radio to listen to the broadcast of the opening ceremony of the Summer Olympics from Berlin. The torchbearer's arrival into the Olympic stadium is greeted by thousands of Germans chanting proudly, 'Sieg Heil! Sieg Heil!' It drowns out the Hallelujah chorus of Handel's 'Messiah'.

Papa listens intently but doesn't say a word as the radio broadcaster describes how the arms of the 100,000-strong crowd are proudly held aloft in the Nazi salute, honouring Hitler who sits in his private box watching on.

Mindla feels sick at the thought and decides to go to bed when the crowd begins chanting 'Heil Hitler, Heil Hitler, Heil Hitler.'

Soon after she arrives at the factory the next morning, Mr Landau calls all of the workers together for a meeting. The machines haven't been cranked up yet and the old cement building is cold, so they huddle up close, eager to hear Mr Landau's news. A chill runs up Mindla's spine when he announces to them all that the Polish Ministry of Commerce has instructed all shop owners to include their name on the signs of their businesses.

He doesn't elaborate, because he doesn't need to; everyone knows what this means. Jewish businesses are being singled out, and before long they will be the target of anti-Semitic attacks. Mr Landau and his workers are in danger.

As she makes her way along rows of sewing machines towards the cutting table, Mindla whispers to the women around her setting out their tools for the day. 'We must all walk home together,' she says. They nod in agreement. This is not the time for any of them to be alone.

Life goes on despite the troubling mood.

Chana's illness continues and she spends more time resting in bed, but on the eve of Rosh Hashanah, Jadzia and Avraham announce they are expecting a baby and the news that she is going to be a grandmother lifts Chana's spirits. She waltzes around the kitchen as she prepares the New Year feast. With the money Mindla earns from Mr Landau's factory and a few precious zlotys her sons-in-law give her each week, she plans a special celebration.

On every floor of 17 Muranowska Street, ovens are stoked in preparation for the New Year festivities. The sweet smell of raisin challah, fresh from the oven, wafts through the apartment building and across the cobblestone square.

It is at special times like this that Mindla misses Kubush the most; she remembers watching Shara's eyes light up when he 'found' a coin behind her ear, or Menachem's face slowly turn red as he held his breath while trying to juggle whatever goodies Kubush brought with him, an apple or two or sometimes a pear.

'Don't you bruise my precious apples!' Chana would yell.

As the autumn weeks roll towards winter Mindla counts down to the circus touring season coming to an end. On the second night of Rosh Hashanah the family gather around Mama's table for dinner. The candles are lit and after Kiddush they pass Chana's golden challah around the table.

Menachem dips his bread in the precious honey and ever so slowly licks off every drop. It is not the traditional way of eating challah but no-one can deny the boy the pleasure when they see his grin from ear to ear. Shara follows everything her big brother does and she too licks the honey off her challah, much to Chana's horror.

'Children! Enough. Behave.'

When everyone has eaten their bread, she quietly slides the little honey bowl in front of Menachem and turns a blind eye while he licks it clean. Laloshe brings a bag of cherries for Chana. They are the last of the summer season's crop and past their best, but perfect to make wisniak. It has been years since Chana has made the delicious sweet wine for Passover. She invites Eva, Jadzia and Mindla to help her.

The women gather around the kitchen table and each takes a pile of cherries, cutting them carefully, discarding their pips, then layering the ruby-red halves inside large glass bottles until the bottles are about three-quarters full.

A little sugar and a good swig of alcohol are added to kick-start the fermenting, then the bottles are sealed up. Chana lines them along the kitchen windowsill. The morning sunlight catches the brew and casts a pretty red reflection across the table. The cherries will slowly ferment over the next few months before being strained and re-bottled as the delicious wine.

It is the first occasion Chana has asked her daughters to help her. 'It's time you learnt how to make this for your own husbands,' she says.

The girls treasure this day, because in their hearts they know that time is running out. Chana barely spends a full day out of bed now and has a cough that makes her whole body convulse. Not even the most foul of Mrs Feigelblum's concoctions is taking the badness from her blood.

Golden leaves form a thick carpet along the banks of the Vistula as the oaks, poplars, elms and willows herald the arrival of another autumn. Despite the punishing winds whipping along the river, a few leaves somehow cling to their branches.

Any day now the circus will roll back into town and Kubush will be home. Mindla dreams of them being together and beginning their married life properly, of his laughter and the way he kisses her. Oh, how she longs for his kisses.

She thinks about their wedding and their visits to the circus; sometimes she can even smell the straw of the stables and hear him whispering in her ear.

She thinks about him as much as she can, to take her mind off the sadness at home.

The doctor now comes regularly. They know it is serious because Papa closes the bedroom door behind him, shielding his children from whatever bad news is being delivered to Mama. A bucket is permanently by her bed, full of bloody rags.

Chana Levin slips away quietly one night on the eve of winter. Mindla wakes to the low hum of Papa's voice and she knows in her heart that her precious Mama is gone. Papa is sitting in their room reciting his psalms, a sheet draped over Chana's ravaged body to protect her dignity.

Shara sleeps soundly on a mattress in the corner of their room, oblivious.

Tiny red lines fill Papa's blue eyes and without any words Mindla knows what has to be done. She puts the kettle on and makes Papa tea, then wakes Eva.

Mindla takes Papa's place in the chair beside Chana and continues to read the psalms while Papa warms himself by the fire. The body of this once robust woman seems so small and pitiful under a shroud. She knew that time was running out for Mama, but still her death breaks her heart.

Was it consumption or typhus? Maybe cancer?

It doesn't matter. Mama is gone.

CHAPTER SIX

Warsaw, Winter 1937

When Kubush returns to Warsaw, he doesn't come alone.

From a distance Mindla can see what she thinks is a child helping him feed the horses at the stables. She is shocked to see a bluish trail of cigarette smoke drift above the boy's head as he sucks on sweet tobacco.

'You'll catch fire one day,' Kubush teases the child, and flicks a handful of straw at his face.

'Alta kaka' – *old shit* – the boy curses back.

Mindla is appalled by the language from someone so young. She is about to give the foul-mouthed urchin a good talking to when Kubush spots her.

'Here she comes!' Kubush says, beaming as she makes her way towards them. 'Faivel, this is my wife, Mindla.'

'This is Faivel?' Mindla says, a little stunned but trying not to be rude as she reaches the pair who are propped up against the wooden gates of the stallion's box.

Faivel Ditkowski, or Faivel Lilliput as he is known on

stage, is Kubush's new circus partner, and although Mindla has heard a lot about Faivel from Kubush's letters he left out a few pertinent details: that Faivel is a chain-smoking dwarf who can swear in four different languages.

'Mindla,' Faivel says, bowing, 'you are more beautiful than your husband describes. How such a fine woman could have married this tuchus – *ass* – is beyond me.'

Kubush grins and wraps his arms around his wife. 'I must be the luckiest man in the world.'

Dinner around the Levins' table is not the same without Chana. There is a heaviness that has descended on the room; an unspoken loss.

That night Kubush attempts to lighten the mood by regaling the family with stories of circus life and his partner Faivel. He recounts how he first met Faivel backstage after curtain close when Faivel was enjoying a whisky with the clowns. The Staniewskis had known him for years and whenever they visited Bialystok, Faivel would distribute posters around town for them in return for tickets to the show. 'What he lacked in height, he made up for in charm,' Kubush chuckles, 'and Lala in particular had a soft spot for him. He'd leave a bouquet of field flowers by her dressing room door.'

Kubush does not mention that Bronislaw is also fond of Faivel because he is reliable and well connected. If the ringmaster needs anything done in Bialystok – a favour from the local mayor or a pile of steaming elephant shit carted away – Faivel is his man. No task is too small or too great.

With their business growing, Faivel was just the sort of help the Staniewski brothers needed on the ground: a trusted set of eyes and ears. So, Faivel was given a job, but he clearly had no intention of remaining the circus gopher for long. He had ambitions, he was smart and worked twice as hard as any other man at the circus.

'When the circus train rolled out of Bialystok, I invited Faivel to share my gypsy caravan. It wasn't long before we had conjured up a new act to impress the Staniewskis.'

The act, which they debuted shortly afterwards, involved Kubush bursting through the curtain dressed as a court jester being chased by Faivel, who was in turn being chased by Mimi the chimpanzee.

It was an easy laugh.

After their first appearance, they then suddenly burst into the arena again in the middle of the ringmaster's introductions, or during Bim and Bom's magic act.

None of which was random, of course, but to the audience's eye the hapless pair being chased in circles by a galloping chimpanzee was hilarious and got funnier as the show went on. Buoyed by their success, Kubush and Faivel kept coming up with new ideas and polished up the perfect slapstick routine. Faivel, playing the bumbling clown, 'accidentally' knocked over a pole supposedly holding up the side of the circus tent. Panic would ensue. Kubush, angry and annoyed with his clumsy colleague, picked up the long piece of wood and spun it around, missing Faivel's head by milli-metres. The audience roared with laughter when Kubush suddenly turned back, swinging the pole in the opposite direction, making his sidekick duck once more. They both had a natural flair for the art of slapstick and the more the audience laughed at the pair's madcap blunders and near misses, the more the Staniewskis loved them.

'We spent hours perfecting new tricks and routines,' Kubush tells the rapt family, their eyes sparkling for the first time since Chana died. 'We often tried them out on Lala Staniewska. Lala has seen just about every circus act there is, and we knew if we could impress her we would get a laugh from the audience. Lala loved it so much and we were so successful on the summer tour, the Staniewskis have invited us to perform at Ordynacka Street during the winter season in Warsaw. We will be "carpet clowns", playing a bit part entertaining the audience in between the main acts, but this is still a big deal – my debut under the domed roof of the prestigious theatre.'

Kubush pauses dramatically. 'And now we are back once more for the winter in Warsaw. You must all be my guests!'

On his first night performing in Warsaw, Kubush arranges tickets for the Levins to see the show, and he invites Mindla backstage to watch him get ready. This is a special night and she is his good-luck charm.

47

Since his return, the young couple have spent every minute together making up for lost time.

Kubush is supposed to live with the Staniewskis and their troupe in Warsaw while they're rehearsing, but Lala has a soft spot for him and bends the rules because the couple are still newlyweds. Every performer is considered one of the extended Staniewski family, so they are treated with generosity and care. In return the Staniewskis expect their stars to work hard and abide by their rules. After every performance, parties, drinking or celebratory carry-on is strictly forbidden. Lala considers rest essential for the performers to be at their physical peak again the next day. However, she makes an exception when the touring troupe gathers to celebrate the end of the long season on the road.

In Warsaw at the prestigious Ordynacka Street theatre, the circus is awake well before dawn every day ready for 6 am rehearsals. Bronislaw and Mieczyslaw Staniewski demand perfection and they rehearse and rehearse until it is achieved. Every performer is required at rehearsal, not just to practise their routines for the next show, but to continually develop new acts, to keep the circus fresh. The Staniewskis insist that every season must offer something new and exciting.

They rehearse until 1 pm, after which they are allowed free time, but no-one is allowed to leave the vicinity of the circus without Lala's specific approval. All performers must be on time for their act. That means dressed and ready to the minute of the official running sheet, no excuses.

On his nights off, Kubush is allowed to stay at Muranowska Street with Mindla, and on other nights Mindla is invited to stay with him at the Staniewskis' apartment as long as she doesn't interrupt rehearsals. Mindla sits quietly in the corner of the clowns' dressing room.

She recognises Bim and Bom, and Sym and Ivan Radunski – the circus's most famous clowns – who all jostle for mirror space, and a cast of colourful characters buzzes around in the background. Each performer arrives a mere mortal but leaves with the power to make magic.

Tonight, the clowns share their dressing room with fourteen children – an acrobat troupe from Abyssinia who dance with snakes and swallow fire. Through a haze of cigarette smoke, Mindla watches Kubush prepare. She finds his transformation mesmerising. He gently drags the soft pink crayon over his skin then blends it around his forehead, up into his blond curls and down his neck. The crayon creates a smooth canvas for the crucial layers to follow, and simultaneously holds the next layer in place while buffering his face from the ghostly stain that the white paint otherwise leaves.

Once the crayon is set, Kubush takes a brush and paints a layer of chalky white emulsion all over his face. Like an artist, he sweeps the badger's hair brush along his jawline with the sort of precision that can only be mastered after years of practice: not too little and not too much, so his face is white and not grey, allowing time for the make-up to set before the next coat.

His eyebrows have now disappeared, virtually glued to his forehead by a thick layer of sticky white face paint that forms the perfect mask. With a steady hand he takes a stick of bright rouge and draws a wide circle on the tip of his nose, before colouring it in. Then, smiling as widely as he can, he draws lines around the perimeter of his mouth. He carefully extends each corner of his lower lip into a wide banana-shaped smile, white paint disguising his top lip; clowns don't have upper lips because it makes them look sad, he tells Mindla when she asks.

The eyes are next. Using a thick kohl pencil, he draws an arch from the bridge of his nose to the outer corner of his eye, then again on the opposite side, making two exaggerated eyebrows. He checks the mirror to make sure they are even, then fills them in.

The finishing touch is a small vertical line drawn in the middle of his eyelids with a corresponding line below that forms a smiling cross when his eyes are opened wide. Once done, he pours some talc onto a soft white powder puff and dusts a layer over his face to set the make-up. After years of practice the whole transformation takes no more than fifteen minutes.

'Voilà,' he says, leaning over and planting a powdery kiss on Mindla's nose.

Tonight's outfit is his favourite, a pair of oversized pants with pillar-box-red and green-apple checks, held up by matching red suspenders, with a pair of wide brown leather shoes with ballooning toes, so big they could have been made for a giant. He fits the balding skull cap tightly onto his head and squeezes his hands.

Mindla laughs hysterically as the flap of fluffy green hair on top suddenly shoots off his head.

Two invisible wires are attached to a cap and threaded through a coat that Kubush wears over the top of the pants. The wires tuck neatly in his hands, so that he can work the device. He is certain Menachem and Shara will love it.

Now fully transformed, the artist is ready for his audience.

Mindla's family fill almost an entire row as they eagerly await Kubush's Ordynacka Street debut. Shmuel sits next to Mindla, his eyes fixed to the heavens, taking in the stunning chandeliers. He didn't want to come, but the family insisted this is just what he needs after Mama's death.

Jadzia with her swelling belly squeezes alongside Menachem and Avraham, Eva and Laloshe look after Minya, and little Shara sits on Sonia's knee beside Yakov.

For two hours they laugh until their tummies hurt.

They grimace when brave Cliff Aeros rides his motorbike into a steel ball cage chased by marauding lions and tigers. Yakov's heart skips a beat at the glamorous trapeze women soaring through the sky in a dazzling rainbow of sequins and feathers, and Menachem's mouth is open so wide his tonsils almost pop out when pretty Edy Rut, the American pilot, appears in her miniature plane performing aerobatic tricks around the roof of the arena.

'Nothing good comes from a clown, does it, Papa?' Mindla says, nudging her father.

'Nothing good comes from a clown, Mindla,' he agrees. Then smiles.

CHAPTER SEVEN

29 August 1937

The lumpy straw mattress doesn't offer Mindla any respite from the unusually humid summer's night. It has been months since Mindla has seen Kubush and she tosses and turns: sheet off, then sheet on again when the mosquitoes find their way to her sticky skin.

The towel beside her is damp with mopped-up sweat.

Every now and then a night delivery horse clops along the cobblestones, offering a welcome distraction from the thoughts keeping her awake and the niggling pain in her abdomen.

All at once a sudden gush of water runs down her legs, confirming that the discomfort has nothing to do with the intemperate Warsaw night. A new chapter in her life is about to begin.

'Yakov, the baby is coming,' she says, gently shaking awake her sleeping brother in the next bed. 'Please run and get Jadzia.'

Yakov snaps out of his bleary-eyed state and races downstairs as fast as his legs will carry him to Jadzia and Avraham's new apartment on Podwale Street. Jadzia has taken to motherhood like a duck to water and has promised she'll be by Mindla's side when her turn comes.

By the time they arrive back, Mindla is doubled over in exactly the same pain she'd seen her mother endure so many times, and Jadzia six months earlier when she had baby Siva.

Jadzia quickly gets the house organised, instructing Minya to get the hot water on and towels ready while pulling blankets off Mindla's bed to make a nest on the kitchen floor. Yakov is then shooed out the door to fetch the doctor. Papa too wisely heads off to his workshop; a man has no place in the kitchen while a baby is being born.

Eva squeezes Mindla's hand and rubs her back. 'Your baby is coming, Mindla!'

Long after the morning sun heralds a new day, a baby boy squeals his way into the world.

'Congratulations, Mindla,' the doctor says, holding the child upside down to get the muck from his lungs, 'he's a good one, strong.'

Jadzia sponges the baby while the doctor checks him over, then wraps him up in a blanket. His work with them is done and he heads off to his daily rounds checking on patients with consumption and typhus. Kubush is away on the summer tour, but Yakov races off to get word through that a baby son has arrived.

The baby has his father's big blue Prussian eyes and a fine layer of blond hair crowning his pink head. He is almost too good to be true; a picture-perfect little doll wrapped up in a blanket. Mindla cannot take her eyes off him. She gazes at his exquisite pink cheeks and tiny fingers and toes, and that night cuddles him up close beside her, nuzzling her nose into his head while taking in the milky scent of his newborn skin. Kubush will be so proud, she thinks.

Word spreads through 17 Muranowska Street that the baby has arrived and people from the neighbourhood bring cakes, eggs and fruit to celebrate. The family from the floor below even gives a goose. This baby brings great riches.

Eight days after the boy is born the mohel comes to perform the official brit milah. In Kubush's absence, Shmuel and Mindla's brothers-in-law help keep tradition, with Papa proudly cradling his first grandson while the ceremony takes place. Baby Horowitz is formally named Gad (Denis), and welcomed into the world with gusto.

On exactly the same day, another celebration is happening far away across the border in Nuremberg. A party to end all parties, a party fit for a king. The streets of the medieval town drip with flowers, flags, bunting. Pennants and streamers decorate every window, every street lamp and corner.

They are the blood-red flags of the Nazis, along with dozens of lovingly hand-stitched banners of arms, the black swastika carefully appliqued at its heart, draped proudly from every available window around the town square.

Each banner is framed with garlands of brilliant red carnations and geraniums hand-picked for the occasion. The market stalls, which normally sell juicy oranges and dozens of types of thick German sausage, are today laden with anti-Semitic souvenirs. The men of the SS queue up at the stalls in their immaculate black uniforms, patiently waiting for a chance to pick up something special to take home. The Greater German Bookshop is doing a roaring trade in Hitler's manifesto and cartoon postcards mocking Jews. The business of hate is booming.

Tens of thousands of people cram into the old town square as Wagner's overtures blare through speakers suspended from the walls of the fourteenth-century church, the Frauenkirche. The Nazi faithful feverishly wait to catch a glimpse of the mighty Führer. Göring and Goebbels mill around chatting, greeting the excited crowd. The Sturmabteilung, the Nazi Party's Sturmabteilung (SA) paramilitary wing in brown uniform, stand guard. And then *he* arrives.

Borrowing all of the pomp and pageantry of a royal coronation, Hitler appears in an open-topped car and steps onto a red carpet, saluting the crowd. Women cry, men raise their arms in awe, no-one dares *not* be moved to tears by his presence. Hitler's blonde-haired maidens, the League of German Girls, hand out lavish gift bags of food to the adoring crowd and members of the Wehrmacht, the armed forces, who fill the back rows as Hitler himself slowly makes his way past his awe-struck subjects. After he greets the crowd, the parade begins.

The rhythmic crunch of leather boots goosestepping across the cobblestone street echoes around the square. Flags are raised high in a show of Aryan might. One hundred journalists from around the world witness the carefully orchestrated show, wiring the images back to foreign lands.

It is the same the following evening. Three hundred thousand people gather at nearby Zeppelin Field for the annual Nazi rally and Hitler's special address. They stand with flags aloft in the darkness, under a striking 'Cathedral of Light', a powerful curtain created by anti-aircraft search-lights that have been lined up to shoot thick beams of light directly into the night sky.

The light pillars pierce the blackness to dazzling effect.

The crowd sings, cheers and forms a human swastika to the drum roll of Wagner's *Rienzi*. They have much to celebrate. In July Germany completed building the Buchenwald camp with its electrified barbed-wire fence and automatic machine-gun sentries, ready to house Hitler's 'guests'.

The Staniewski Bros Circus has been performing to a packed big-top tent in Czestochowa, the city where pilgrims descend once a year to celebrate the Feast of the Black Madonna, the mother saint of Poland. They come from every corner of

Poland to the Jasna Gora Monastery, many walking, some on their knees, just to take a glimpse of the centuries-old painting of a black-skinned Virgin Mary, which they believe has the power to perform miracles.

'Look at all of the people here to celebrate the arrival of the son of Horowitz!' Kubush joked to Faivel when they first arrived, heading straight for the synagogue to make special prayers for the arrival of his precious firstborn son.

Kubush has walked a little bit taller since that day. He shares his news with everyone he passes. 'I have a baby boy!' he says, with a smile wider than anything he can paint on. The thought of holding his child carries him through the long weeks until he will be home.

The circus moves on to Krakow, then Katowice and finally Lwow, where Kubush is able to share the news of the baby's arrival with his father.

Over a shot or two of wisniak, Kubush regales his father with stories of circus life and his beautiful young bride. They reminisce about their own lives and pray for the future of the baby. Mendel shares wise words about fatherhood – with eight children he's had enough practice to know.

Kubush's stepmother makes him promise to be good to his wife, to look after her. The house is noticeably quieter without Albert and Jakub, who have joined the Polish army and are now training somewhere near Warsaw. Mendel Horowitz is worried about what trouble his boys will find themselves in and pleads with Kubush to keep an eye on them. Kubush agrees and before he leaves hugs his father and promises that he will visit when the circus tours next time. Maybe he'll be able to bring Mindla and the baby to visit too, he says.

'I'd like that,' his father replies and smiles, but Kubush notices the tears in his eyes before he turns and walks away.

PART II
War

CHAPTER EIGHT

August 1939, Bialystok

One by one, the many wagons of the Cyrk Staniewski roll once more into Bialystok to prepare for its stint in Poland's eastern border city. It is mid-August, and Kubush misses Gad, who is growing up so fast between visits. He thinks back to the first time he laid eyes on his adored son. It was late in the evening when he arrived home from the long circus tour and Gad was sound asleep, curled up so peacefully. Kubush laid down beside the sleeping child and gently stroked his angelic freckled face until he nodded off too. Finally he was home and with his family.

Kubush's reverie is interrupted by Faivel opening the brittle pine shutters of their caravan just far enough to flick another smouldering cigarette out onto the dusty potholed roads around Biala Podlaska.

'You stumpy-legged schmuck, one day you'll send us up in flames,' Kubush teases.

As he and Faivel are bumped and rocked along the

winding dirt roads to Bialystok, Kubush daydreams of long walks through the lush gardens of the city's Branicki Palace, stretching his legs and soaking in a lungful of fresh air.

In past visits, he's managed to sneak away from the circus with his lunch bag and lie out on the palace lawns, soaking up the sun. Some days he'll curl up under the shady arms of a linden tree for a few blessed minutes' shut-eye before the afternoon rehearsal. Kubush promises himself that he will bring Mindla and Gad here one day. He often wonders if they could make it their home. Mindla would love the gilded baroque mansion, and little Gad could accompany him on adventures into the nearby Bialowieza Forest, fishing and hunting. Legend has it that lynx and mongooses are so abundant in the ancient forest you can almost reach out and touch them, if you dare. And enormous bison, the size of a small truck, roam free.

Bialystokers love the Staniewski Bros Circus, and dozens of excited children run alongside the colourful procession cheering and waving as the wagons arrive in town. Kubush always feels at home in Bialystok; the cobblestone streets and wooden cottages remind him of Lwow.

The circus is set up at Plac Wyzwolenia, Liberation Square, in the heart of the city, alongside the railway tracks. They are close enough to the Biala river that during his breaks, Kubush can wander along the stream and dip his toes in the water. On their days off, some of the clown troupe even dare to swim. Lala would kill them if she knew.

The last time the Cyrk Staniewski rolled into town they hoisted three giant big-top tents to accommodate the packed crowd. This year, the circus has been so popular Bronislaw Staniewski has added another tent to their empire. Four soaring canvas big tops that will completely overshadow any rival who dares to take him on. Staniewski Brothers is the biggest and the best in Poland.

With the talk of war all around, the circus is just what is needed to lift the spirits and provide an evening of distraction, and there is no end of able-bodied helpers willing to assist in lifting the four huge big tops into the sky. It takes almost two days to get the tents erected, bleachers locked in place and the arena ready for rehearsal. With the circus flags proudly flying above the Bialystok skyline, ticket sales are swift and it looks like the troupe are going to have a sell-out on their hands. While Kubush and the others are helping put the finishing touches to the marquee decorations, Faivel is busy distributing posters and flyers all around town. This is his hometown, and he knows every nook and cranny.

After two days walking the streets, sticking and posting, there isn't a shop window or telegraph pole that doesn't feature the smiling faces of the new, exotic Japanese trapeze artists the Ohojos, or the pretty Italian gymnasts in their feathered costumes.

Faivel's work pays off and by the time the shutters of the box office caravan are hooked back each evening, a queue has already formed.

'Latecomers will miss out, the audience is bursting under the four-tent big top,' the local newspaper writes after opening night.

The highlight of this season's bill is Maestro Watson, an illusionist and magician who has electricity running through his veins and can light up cigarettes, light bulbs and torches by 'sheer force of will'.

Word quickly spreads about Maestro and his magic fingers and people come from miles around to see for themselves. After a week of sell-out shows, the performance on Thursday 31 August will be their last before a few days' break. Friday is the start of the Sabbath and as a third of the Bialystok population is Jewish, Bronislaw knows it is a good time for everyone to rest.

Faivel's family invite Kubush to spend the Sabbath with them.

The Thursday show begins at 8:30 pm on the dot with the orchestra's thundering version of *Entrance of the Gladiators*. Backstage it is the cue: showtime.

As usual, the horses and chimpanzees are a popular warm-up act, giving the audience a tantalising taste of what is to come. The Ohojo twins prove an instant hit. The talented gymnasts fly through the sky at great speed, swinging high into the cupola as the audience claps along to a rousing version of Chopin's *Mazurka*. A death-defying trapeze act. But it is Maestro Watson they have all come to see.

In act one, he strides out into the arena with his glamorous assistant, who is carrying a fancy silver tray in her hands. One lone cigarette sits in the middle of the shiny platter. The blonde assistant takes the tray over to the audience and allows everyone to take a close look, touch or feel the little papieros. She walks back to Maestro, who is very dramatically standing under the full glare of the spotlight in the arena, and she hands him the cigarette. Maestro puts the thin white tobacco roll to his lips, then shakes his arms and legs out to show the audience there are no matches or trickery up his sleeves.

As the audience falls completely silent, he stretches his arm out and gently touches a fingertip to the end of the cigarette. Within seconds, it begins to smoulder and a thin grey plume of smoke floats into the air. Maestro, grinning madly as his teeth hold the cigarette in place, laps the arena so everyone can see for themselves, then hands the cigarette to a young man in the front row who happily smokes it to its butt. 'Bravo!' they cheer.

This is Maestro's entree. With the touch of a fingertip Maestro Watson turns on a light bulb, then makes a torch shine brighter than the audience has ever seen. His magic fingers bring everything he touches to life.

A buzz sweeps through the big top. The audience knows what is coming, it is the very reason they've paid seven precious zlotys to be here. Maestro's energy fills the air and the anticipation builds. His assistant rolls out the pièce de résistance of his act, an electric chair from America, the same used to execute prisoners on death row. Gasps can be heard from the audience as the lethal brown wooden chair is locked into place.

Maestro then lowers himself into the chair as his assistant straps his wrists and ankles. She plugs the chair into an electric generator. Wires are placed all over his body. For some, it is too much to watch. The ramifications if this goes wrong are too ghastly to contemplate. Electric volts surging through his body will instantly fry his brain and heart. Encouraged by the audience's fear, Maestro begins a maudlin countdown, willing the audience to count along with him.

'Ten, nine, eight, seven . . .' they chant in unison.

At zero, his trusted assistant flicks the 'on' switch. Seconds later the chair lights up, sparks fly and the audience screams in horror. Maestro is being electrocuted.

After a few agonising moments, the switch is flicked off and the once lifeless-looking figure miraculously stands up from the chair, steps forward and takes a triumphant bow. 'But how?' they wonder. 'How did he survive?'

A few moments later the audience begins an impromptu chorus for an encore. 'Repeat, repeat, repeat,' they chant. But there is no encore. Being fried alive once tonight is enough for the clever illusionist.

Maestro is a hard act to follow.

The following day, the newspaper describes his as 'The most exciting act!', 'Breathtaking', and comments, 'Thunderous applause for Maestro Watson'. But the real genius of course is Bronislaw Staniewski, who signed Maestro to perform. Maestro has not only lit up light bulbs, he has lit up the ticket box too.

It is almost midnight by the time the performers have cleaned up after the show, fed the animals and settled in for bed. Although alcohol is forbidden, Faivel has a bottle of whisky tucked under his straw mattress for special occasions, and after a long day, knowing they have a few days off, Faivel and Kubush share a nip or three.

Word soon spreads and one or two others join them too. As the night wears on, they toast their friends, they toast their families and glorious Poland, and they curse Hitler, 'szalony kutas!' – *mad prick!*

After a rousing rendition of the Polish national anthem, the merry men drift off to sleep, completely oblivious that Hitler is on his way.

CHAPTER NINE

1 September 1939, Warsaw

The sky is just beginning to turn pink when the noise wakes Mindla. It is a familiar rumble, almost rhythmic, metal scraping on metal followed by a soft thud every now and then, off in the distance.

As the pattern repeats, it doesn't take long to settle in Mindla's mind. Definitely aeroplanes.

She prays it is the Polish Air Force still practising their dogfights and drills. Slivers of sunlight creep through cracks in the paper-thin blinds. Gad is fast asleep beside her, oblivious to the din outside. She cuddles the toddler in close and gently strokes his forehead as she lies in bed listening to the strange noise.

She notices the absence of the pigeons that nest on the window box outside her room, usually cooing among themselves at this time of the morning.

The thunder rolls in, louder and louder and louder.

She pulls back the corner of the blind.

'Oh, good God!' she gasps.

The dawn horizon is dotted with silver birds, their bellies bursting with bombs. A long whining scream is followed by impact and then an explosion. She scoops up the sleeping child and runs into the kitchen.

Mindla's brothers and sisters jostle for position at the windows, watching the horrific sky show. Hitler's Luft-waffe, flying in perfect formation, line the skies as far as their eyes can see. The family hear the screeching noise again, followed by a haunting whistle and then the thud of impact.

'Get down!' Shmuel yells as they each dive under the kitchen table or their beds, cowering.

A few seconds later, before they have time to catch their breath, the same noise, a high-pitched hiss followed by the thump of a bomb smashing into the earth somewhere nearby. Their building judders. For a few moments there is silence, then the wailing of an air-raid siren sparks a frenzied rush.

A human stampede is heard outside the apartment door as neighbours, panic-stricken and shrieking, push and shove their way down the narrow wooden stairs to the cellar.

Shmuel is yelling too. 'Run, we must run!' he cries, but instead of running, they freeze, momentarily unable to process what is going on. Another air-raid siren snaps them into the terrifying reality that Warsaw is under attack.

'Attention, attention,' a loudspeaker screams, 'it comes!'

There is no time to run. Mindla snatches a blanket and throws it underneath her bed, pushing Gad as far into the corner as she can. She crawls in beside him and does her best to shield him with her body from whatever's about to happen.

Sonia does the same with little Shara under the next bed. The little girl puts her fingers in her ears when the bombs' piercing whistles fill the room. In every available spot someone shelters – under the kitchen table, in the closet, under beds – while bomb after bomb rains down on the city. Blitzkrieg has been unleashed.

In the maelstrom, Mindla loses all track of time and has no idea how long they spend trembling under their beds. It feels like an eternity. Sometime later the loud speakers declare the air raid is over.

One by one, shell-shocked neighbours emerge and make their way out onto the street. Mindla dusts herself down and joins them. Although still not confident they are safe, she is comforted by the sight of familiar faces. Miraculously, Muranowska Street remains intact, but others one or two blocks away aren't so lucky. Buildings are on fire. Thick smoke fills the air. The smell of fuel and acrid smoke lines their mouths.

When Mindla returns to their apartment, Yakov has news from the street: Hitler is on his way. While they were sleeping overnight, one million German troops flooded Poland's borders. At 4:45 am they struck. Poland is at war.

It is a lie to say Mindla is surprised.

For months the country has been on edge as the land forces of the Wehrmacht inched towards the border. In her heart, she's hoped nothing bad will happen to her harmless country, but her head knows the truth.

Poland is a defenceless player in a game of political piggy in the middle, a prize to be carved up. The country's fate was sealed the previous month when German foreign minister Joachim von Ribbentrop and Soviet foreign minister Vyacheslav Molotov signed a non-aggression treaty, a secret pact to divide Poland.

Although the dark curtain of war has been lowering menacingly for some time, Mindla has gone about her business as usual, going to the shops and factory each day, desperately hoping the talk of war will dissipate.

In the weeks leading up to invasion, she became quite accustomed to seeing troops on the streets. The sound of Polish fighter aircraft practising manoeuvres in the sky offered comfort, not alarm. The Polish army built anti-aircraft sites around the city and every available man was asked to help dig trenches in parks and gardens to assist the army's efforts.

Posters calling for men to enlist were pinned up on street corners. 'Help them!' and 'Poles to arms!' they cry. Mindla thought at first this was all precautionary, but now she's beginning to realise she underestimated the gravity of the situation.

That afternoon the air-raid sirens begin again. When the sirens howl, Gad howls too. Somehow he knows what is coming. The Levins run to the basement or cower under their beds when it's too late, knowing in their hearts that neither shelter will save them if a bomb directly hits the building.

Mindla hugs her son to her chest and hums nursery rhymes to soothe him, marvelling at how much like his father he looks. How she wishes Kubush were here now.

In the lull between afternoon and evening air raids, Minya sits on the bedroom floor with Gad and Shara singing songs and playing patty cakes, while Mindla tries to finish off the socks she is knitting for Kubush. Mr Landau gave her some scraps of bright-red yarn from the factory that she thinks will match Kubush's costume perfectly. She takes her fear out on the knitting needles, her fingers trying to weave a little piece of normality amid the chaos.

It doesn't last long. As sunset arrives, so too do the Luftwaffe.

CHAPTER TEN

Word reaches Bialystok that Warsaw is under attack. News from a radio broadcast whips around the circus camp with lightning speed. 'Have you heard? Hitler is coming!' they whisper.

Dusk is approaching when the circus managers call the camp together for a briefing. 'You have all heard the devastating news. Until such time as the Polish army can regain our skies, we must suspend our performances. Tomorrow we will pack up the tents and secure our belongings before we make further plans.'

Kubush and Faivel rush off to Faivel's home for Shabbas. It is good to be with his family, and Frida Ditkowski's pierogi are a welcome change from the usual fare served up by the circus cooks, but Kubush can't relax and his mind is constantly on Mindla and Gad.

'She'll be fine,' Faivel says, reading his vacant stare, 'her brothers-in-law will look after her.'

Although it is the Sabbath, there is no rest for the circus.

At dawn, the entire troupe gets to work bringing down the enormous canvas marquees and packing them away. Bleachers are taken apart piece by piece and the animals secured in their caravans. It is decided that as it's too unsafe to travel back to Warsaw at the moment, they will stay in Bialystok until the situation settles.

Warsaw barely whispers, holding its collective breath until the sun comes up again. The squares and markets are deserted.

With each raid, Mindla shelters under the bed, her arm stretched over Gad, curling him against her body, or, when the mortars begin to drop too close, scooping the boy up and running down to the basement. Time and again, dozens of families squeeze into the damp cellar under the building, hoping they'll be spared. They sit in silence. There is nothing to say. Instead, their ears are trained to air-raid sirens, while a crystal-set radio broadcasting news from outside offers a distraction. Mindla never feels safe underground, having heard dreadful stories of cellar doors covered in rubble, suffocating the poor souls inside.

It is a relief when they can head upstairs again.

Out on the streets she tries not to inhale the sickening smell of rotting flesh, fuel, sewage, plaster dust and burning wood – of burning everything – but the air is thick with it day and night. Back in the apartment she is too scared to light a candle, almost too scared to speak, as she's heard Polish soldiers armed with guns running up the stairs banging on the neighbours' doors screaming, 'Turn off your lights! Every light is a target for the enemy! Darkness only!'

Door by door they have enforced a complete blackout. Bombs are now the only thing lighting up Warsaw at night.

Around the world, newspaper headlines announce, 'War! Bombs Rain on Warsaw'. The world knows Poland is under attack and on 3 September, Britain and France declare war on Germany. Mindla heaves a sigh of relief. The Allies are coming to help. After days under siege, the city throngs with people and bursts into song.

The living dead emerge from the earth: from shelters, cellars, from apartments and from the rubble of apartments where they've been hiding. Women with bloodied faces appear, clinging to children covered in dust; men streaked with dirt and blood, their clothes torn apart. The Polish flag flies proudly from balconies and the national anthem, *Poland Is Not Yet Lost*, echoes from the radio. 'Marsz, marsz, Dabrowski,' people sing at the tops of their voices, followed by *God Save the Queen* and *La Marseillaise*. No-one seems to care that they don't know the words. Mindla sings until her throat hurts. The war isn't over, but Poles can steel themselves to endure this nightmare for a few more days until the Allies arrive to chase away the Germans and save them.

In Bialystok, Kubush assumes the city is well prepared should it be attacked by the Wehrmacht. The Polish army has spent the last few months digging trenches and building anti-aircraft bunkers around Wizna, an important strategic village to the west of Bialystok. Wizna is on the main route from Warsaw so the Polish army invested considerable time and manpower into setting up an impenetrable fortification line in the fields around the edge of town. The walls of the bunkers are made of concrete, one-and-a-half metres thick and lined with steel plates for reinforcement. Seven hundred Polish troops are stationed around the region to repel any threat. But they are no match for Hitler, who sends 42,000 of his finest Nazi troops, along with 350 Panzer tanks.

For days the withered Polish forces valiantly fight them off, but on 7 September the village of Wizna is captured. During their retreat, the Poles have cleverly blown up the bridge crossing the Narew river on the road to Warsaw, but it can't stop the Germans forever, it only delays their inevitable advance.

Once the Nazis reach the southern bank of the Narew, their path is clear to encircle Warsaw from the north. After Wizna falls, it is only a matter of time before the Wehrmacht arrive in Bialystok. Each day, ghostly figures emerge from the fields and forests around Bialystok, and men and women who'd fled Warsaw soon after the initial air attacks arrive clinging on to hungry children, searching for shelter and safety.

They bring with them grim news from home, horrific stories about the Luftwaffe's reign of terror over the skies, of bombs and burning, of dead bodies piled up on the street. Of others who haven't made it to Bialystok, gunned down by merciless fighter pilots in open fields and roads as they ran for their lives. Heaven help the poor souls who are on their way now and about to run head-on into the advancing Nazis.

A week after the invasion begins, it isn't the Allies on Warsaw's doorstep, it's the Germans. The Panzer tanks are circling the city and a land battle begins in earnest. Warsaw is now being attacked by air and by land, and there is barely time for a breath between shellfire. Dead bodies, human and horse, litter the streets.

Kind strangers drag the dead into bombed buildings or lay them in trenches; dignity in the absence of a place to bury them. Prayers are said in between gunfire, by way of a makeshift funeral. It is the best anyone can do.

Mindla quickly learns the difference between the smell of a dead human and a rotting horse. It helps to recognise which horror you are about to come across and gives a moment's warning to steel yourself for what lies around the next corner.

After days of constant attack, food is beginning to run scarce. Bread and milk are very hard to come by. From sunrise to after sunset, Yakov and Menachem search the streets for food, bartering and begging. The wily boys manage to dodge shellfire and gather enough to get the family through another day. They queue for hours for a chunk of bread, and sometimes come home with an onion and a potato, on a lucky day some dripping or flour. No-one asks where these morsels come from; they are so hungry they don't care.

In desperation, some people carve chunks of flesh off the dead horses.

Yakov often brings news of the Polish army's success, which he's heard on the grapevine. In an effort to keep up morale, the newspapers and radio boast of the great feats of the Polish army. According to the papers the Polish soldiers are heroic and brave and the army has shot down huge numbers of Luftwaffe.

Mindla can't understand why, if that's true, the radio is calling for citizens to make bandages because the hospitals are running out. Common sense suggests the army's efforts are perhaps not going to plan. She can find very little written about the casualties on Poland's side.

The Germans bomb hospitals, railway lines, telephone lines, roads, schools, banks – anything to strangle Warsaw. Each day Mayor Starzynski's calming voice comes over the crystal-set, reassuring his city's people that the Polish land force is strong and resilient. He asks for everyone to do their bit to help defend the capital.

'Side by side we stand with our neighbours,' he says, promising that the Allies will arrive soon to rescue them. But still they don't come. Mindla begins to wonder if they ever will.

At night, a secret city begins to emerge. Shopkeepers open up under the cover of darkness to distribute whatever food they have left, and people scurry around town checking on relatives and friends before the bombs begin to fall again. Often, Yakov heads out onto the street to find out what is going on or checks on Jadzia and Avraham, who have stayed in their apartment on Podwale Street. One evening, as he rounds the corner into Muranowska on his way home, he walks straight into a group of young men, familiar from around the neighbourhood. They have packs on their backs and determined faces. 'Where are you going?' he asks.

'Haven't you heard? The government is leaving Warsaw.'

Yakov runs. He bursts through the apartment door and spits out words so fast Shmuel can barely understand him. 'But where are they going, Yakov?' Mindla asks, trying to slow the boy down. He shrugs his shoulders. 'East, they say it's safe there.'

Mindla clutches her chest, momentarily buoyed by the news that the east, and therefore Kubush, is safe.

Overnight a human river flows out of the city. Mindla thinks these people are fools, for German planes are tearing up the roads and fields around Warsaw, so they'll be sitting ducks as dawn breaks over Poland. As morning comes, word spreads through the building that the government is setting up its offices in Lublin. Yakov's gossip was correct. It plans to stay for two or three weeks until the Allies help secure Warsaw and it can return.

Rumour has it that French troops are mounting an offensive against Germany from the Maginot Line, forcing Hitler to move his army and his attention there.

On 10 September, a Sunday, Mindla counts seventeen consecutive Luftwaffe raids. She sees no sky that day, only thick, dark smoke extending to the horizon. German aircraft pelt bullets at anything and anyone, showering the streets in wave after wave of attacks. The basement of every apartment building, church and synagogue is full. Some people wear gas masks. Many find refuge in the stairwells of buildings, too frightened they'll be buried alive to hide underground. At night, any number of strangers call the wooden stairs of the Levins' Muranowska Street apartment building home.

Mindla and her family share what they can, blankets or food, even though there is very little of either. Barely a week after the whispers that the German troops would soon retreat, the Luftwaffe brings Warsaw to its bloodied knees, attacking the city's heart. One by one the buildings that define Warsaw and her people are targeted. The first is beloved Royal Castle, which goes up in flames. At 11:15 am, its clock is frozen hauntingly at the time of artillery impact. The breathtaking ceiling of the majestic ballroom collapses, taking artist Marcello Bacciarelli's baroque fresco *The Creation of the World* with it. The castle's staff manage to extinguish the fire before it spreads, but the masterpiece is lost forever.

Then St John's Cathedral, where Poland's kings were crowned and royalty, great composers, artists and writers are buried, is peppered with artillery fire.

The message is loud and clear. Hitler is coming for Warsaw's soul.

'I'm so sorry, Mindla,' Yakov says gently, breaking the worst news yet. 'Ordynacka Street was bombed. The circus building is gone.'

Mindla's heart almost stops. The next morning, she runs.

Even though Nazi pilots are flying so low that they can pinpoint a single human, a woman pushing a pram or running for her life, Mindla runs, numb to the chaos around her.

She needs to see for herself.

The buildings she once wandered past arm in arm with Kubush on the way to the circus are nothing but rubble. The coffee shop where they'd had clandestine dates, a burnt-out shell. She barely recognises her city. By the time she reaches the corner of Ordynacka Street, her lungs are choked with the foul stench of burning. She stops opposite the circus, sheltering in the doorway of a tenement building. The outside of the circus building has miraculously survived, the stone walls blackened from fire but otherwise intact, but a direct hit has gutted the entire complex from the inside.

The domed roof and everything under it, completely gone. The beautiful theatre, the leather seats, the velvet curtains, now a molten mess. The stables have been destroyed along with the animals cowering in them. There is nothing but a smoking, hollowed-out shell, a moon-sized crater where Lala Staniewska once proudly corralled her beautiful white horses. Mindla's knees turn to jelly and her legs suddenly slip out from underneath her. She crumples in the corner of the portico and sobs.

Every day and every night the attacks continue in Warsaw. The Red Cross does its best to help the wounded but it simply can't keep up with the rush of injured seeking help. The Jewish community establishes its own hospital on Zielna Street to help the effort. Friends, neighbours and relatives are buried whenever and wherever they can be, in parks and gardens, anywhere they can find earth to dig. Nevertheless, many are left to rot on the streets.

After three weeks of relentless attacks, the electricity is cut off and there is no more bread to be found. Water is scarce. Mindla is grateful for the horse flesh cut from the slain animals lying in the streets to feed her little boy. And just when she can't imagine the situation getting any worse, the following morning the most intense bombardment begins: more than a thousand attacks, some by air, some by land, in a final push by the Wehrmacht. Mindla, cradling Gad, spends all of that day and night squeezed in the cellar alongside dozens of others. Bodies are jammed together, with only the howl of a small child every now and then letting them know they are alive. They feel every bomb. The earth trembles around them, dusty rubble falls from the roof. The air is a putrid mix of smoke, cigarette smoke, body odour and urine. People are coughing. It's impossible to know if it's from the smoke or disease that is spreading through the ravaged city. If the bombs don't kill them, typhus will.

They survive to see another sunrise and Mindla feels relieved, but wonders what good relief is, when she is under seige and separated from her husband.

CHAPTER ELEVEN

15 September, Bialystok

On Friday 15 September, the second day of Rosh Hashanah, when Jews mark the beginning of a new year, rumour spreads that the Germans have reached the outskirts of Bialystok.

The following morning, they enter the city unopposed.

An endless sea of green uniforms appears on the horizon, their polished black jackboots snapping in crisp unison as they snake through the streets of the city. A convoy of armoured vehicles follows: motorcycles, half-tracks, Panzer tanks and trucks. It is an impressive show of force. Their rendezvous point is the town square, which by now is bursting with military personnel and their death machines.

For several days after the Nazis arrive, Bialystok is eerily quiet, lulling everyone into a false sense of security. A curfew was imposed from day one, requiring the streets to be clear from sunset until dawn. But peace doesn't last long.

On the eve of Yom Kippur, the most solemn and holy day for Jews, a twelve-year-old boy is shot dead for being on the street five minutes after curfew. The child was running home from Jewish school when he was shot in the back. The callous murder sparks an outbreak of violence. The Nazis shoot anyone who looks at them sideways.

One afternoon a low-flying bomber drops thousands of leaflets over the city. Kubush picks one up. Written in Belarusian, the propaganda slips tell the citizens of Bialystok that the city will soon be 'liberated' by the Red Army. The Soviets are on their way.

This is, of course, all planned, part of Ribbentrop and Molotov's pact. The Germans secure the city then retreat for the Russians to take over, with Bialystok now falling behind the new Soviet border.

In their last days in Bialystok, the German troops go on a wild looting spree, storming homes and stealing anything precious they can get their hands on. They raid the city's famous textile factories and steal clothing and blankets, more than their arms can carry. Their trucks are stuffed with boxes of food and the treasures of others. No prize too big or too small. Women are stopped on the street and ordered to take off their wedding rings or be shot.

No-one doubts the Nazis' ability to carry out the threat.

During their six days in Bialystok, the Germans kill more than a hundred people and vandalise and loot more than two hundred Jewish factories and homes. As quickly as they arrive, they march out of town.

•

Word spreads quickly when the long Soviet convoy appears on the horizon. Local officials rally townsfolk to prepare a welcome worthy of their saviours. People dress in their finest clothes – Poles, Jews, everyone – and line the streets of Bialystok, clapping and cheering as the tanks roll in.

Women and children throw flowers at the troops, creating a pretty carpet of garden blooms for the Red Army's arrival. Flowers are tossed into the turrets of tanks, young girls hug infantrymen who are happy to reciprocate. A sense of joy and celebration sweeps through the town.

The Russians immediately brand their new city. Huge posters of Stalin are unfurled. Red flags with the familiar golden hammer and sickle are hoisted up every flagpole and draped from every available window. People decorate their homes with anything red they can find as a show of goodwill. The colour of bloodshed and murder is now the colour of hope and peace.

On the afternoon of 27 September Mayor Starzynski's familiar voice is heard over radios across Warsaw. 'Citizens,' he says dolefully, a tone far from the rousing bellow he's used for his morale-boosting missives each day. 'Here speaks Warsaw for the last time.' He takes a slow breath between each sentence, trying not to choke on his words. 'Today at 12 pm a ceasefire has been reached . . .'

This isn't news to be celebrating. The Germans have overrun the Polish army and the government has surrendered.

The mayor pleads with his people to keep calm, and calls upon them to be stoic and remain orderly during food distribution.

'Warsaw on fire. Warsaw in blood. Warsaw in tears,' he says.

Then silence.

The next voice they hear through the radio is that of General Erwin Rommel urging the Polish Army to surrender with dignity. 'I rely on the population of Warsaw, which stood bravely in its defence and displayed its profound patriotism, to accept the entry of German forces quietly, honourably and calmly.'

Warsaw and her people belong to the Nazis.

CHAPTER TWELVE

Warsaw

The bombing finally stops but the silent skies offer no real relief from the horror. No-one sleeps, knowing they are no longer free. People cautiously emerge from battered buildings and dank basements, eager to stretch their legs and fill their lungs. For once, the bitter taste of the burning city makes a pleasant change from the putrid smell of unwashed humans. The autumn sun on Mindla's back warms her.

Warsaw is unrecognisable from the city she knows.

Whole streets are gone. She finds craters where a house once stood, and mountains of rubble line the streets. Sometimes a stiff arm or a bloodied leg pokes out from underneath the debris, sometimes a dusty teddy bear.

One day, as she carefully steps around a mountain of brick, a bluish speck catches Mindla's eye. She stops and pushes away the dirt to find a china teacup; pretty little blue cornflowers dot its rim. It is dirty but otherwise perfectly intact. She assumes the teacup's owners haven't been so lucky. She carefully tucks the precious treasure inside her bag; it is now her good-luck charm. She reasons if that fragile teacup can survive, so can she.

Food is impossibly hard to come by. There are no new supplies coming in, no peasants farming, no carts bringing deliveries from the provinces around Warsaw. Mindla's fingers are weaved tight through Gad's hands as they navigate the streets searching for food. Naturally, he wants to climb the piles of rubble to play, blissfully unaware of the horrors they hide. He is annoyed that she doesn't give him an inch to move away from her side. People take pity on a woman alone with a child. Sometimes they'll offer a piece of bread or an onion, and she is always grateful. On a lucky day, Yakov brings home a chunk of horse fat.

Mindla boils up a pot of soup flavoured with the horse fat and sparingly tosses in just enough of their dwindling portion of kasha so that the buckwheat thickens the grey liquid. This soup must last them several days.

Every waking minute is consumed with the search for food and water, and everyone takes a turn hunting any morsels to survive. The banks of the Vistula are only a short walk from the Levins' apartment but they've been warned not to drink from the river because it is full of rotting bodies. Instead, they scour the streets for a pump that works and fill anything they can carry – a pot, a bucket, even their hot water bottles – with the liquid gold. Long queues form when a working hydrant is found, with people standing in line for hours to collect some clean water.

Rich or poor, they are all in the same situation. No matter how much money you have, you can't buy food if there's no food to buy.

On 1 October the German army arrives. The sight of Hitler's troops marching through the streets sends a chill up Mindla's spine but she joins the crowds lining the roads, alongside Yakov and Sonia, to witness this poisonous parade. The German national anthem bellows through loudspeakers. 'Deutschland, Deutschland über alles – *Germany, Germany above all –*' over and over again as thousands of Wehrmacht boots stomp past, followed by the black-clad SS and their dogs. Some of the neighbours sing along with gusto, proudly waving Nazi flags.

Despite the bloody battle to capture Poland, the Wehrmacht arrive with helmets shining, boots polished to mirror perfection, and not a speck of dust on their uniforms. Mindla wonders how they can be so clean.

A long line of Panzer tanks, motorbikes mounted with machine guns, trucks and heavy artillery follows the soldiers. The earth trembles as they roll by. Row after row of stiff-lipped young men march past. Mindla studies their faces hoping to catch a glimpse of warmth or empathy somewhere, but she is met with glassy eyes that stare straight through her. It is now obvious why the well-intentioned Polish forces, their ranks filled by men conscripted off the streets, were never a match for this terrifyingly disciplined might.

•

The Germans waste no time establishing their authority. Curfews are immediately imposed; no-one is to be on the streets at night. Then, just before dawn the next morning, the neighbourhood is woken with what is to become a familiar cry. 'Raus, raus', the Germans scream – *out, out.*

With whips in hand and pistols cocked, they drag men from their beds to form labour gangs, tasked with cleaning up the city. The men have no tools, just bare hands and the butt of a rifle at their backs, but they work all day throwing bricks, moving rubble, dragging bits of rotting bodies and burning horse carcasses. The Nazis sit and watch.

By the end of the first day every man knows the Nazis' rules: argue and be shot. The desperate clean-up is not for the good of the Polish people or to restore dignity and order to Warsaw, it is in preparation for the arrival of Hitler himself.

Five days later the Führer and his entourage arrive for a victory parade, a brash show of the Reich's might. Thousands of soldiers line the boulevard of Aleje Ujazdowskie, cheering and enthusiastically waving red Nazi flags. Bunting drips from every visible window and ribbon garlands ensure Hitler's stage is fit for a king. An endless sea of troops, horses and artillery triumphantly marches in time to a German brass band that plays their national anthem and Hitler's favourite Wagner compositions. This is a great celebration.

Row after row of soldiers goosestep past the Führer and his generals, their arms locked proudly in the Nazi salute, their feet snapping in perfect rhythm. It is no coincidence that his podium is erected directly opposite the United States Embassy. Hitler is thumbing his nose at the western world.

It is undoubtedly a stunning victory parade, a gloriously orchestrated show of German fanfare and unquestionable power. After the main parade Hitler is driven through the city propped up in an open-topped convertible car, waving to his new subjects. He sweeps past the towering St Alexander's Church, the Rembielinskiego Palace, the Belvedere Palace, beautiful buildings miraculously still standing and now at his disposal. Then the motorcade moves down Nowy Swiat, one of the main historic thoroughfares in Warsaw where, unbeknown to him, the Polish resistance plan to assassinate him. They have earlier that day lined a street with explosives, but for some reason they don't go off.

Oblivious, the Führer waves to his adoring crowds all the way to a nearby airstrip where an aircraft is waiting to take him back to Berlin.

Hitler's visit is the signal for his men to begin unleashing a brutal campaign to rid Poland of its Jews. Mindla is terrified. Orthodox Jews are being beaten and humiliated on the streets, with elderly men having their beards painfully hacked off with knives. The bank accounts of all Jews are immediately frozen, leaving some families with only whatever money they have in their pockets.

Propaganda posters linking Jews with typhus and disease are pinned up around the streets. 'Achtung! Seuchengefahr!'

Warning! Beware of epidemic hazards! In other words, stay away from Jews. Warnings about the Jews are repeatedly echoed in German and Polish through loudspeakers around the city. The SS prowl the streets in packs waiting for an opportunity to shoot a Jew dead or beat him to within an inch of his life; a glance in the wrong direction or a man unaware he is no longer allowed to walk the same street as the Germans is all it takes. German shepherd dogs strain at their leashes to maul a filthy Jew.

One by one, Wehrmacht trucks pull up in the streets of wealthy Jewish families, and troops ransack the homes for furniture, crockery and even curtains. Sometimes the soldiers stand back, guns cocked, and insist the owners themselves carry a much-loved dining table or sofa outside to the waiting trucks that will deliver the items to a 'deserving' Nazi commander. Their belongings are a 'gift' for the Germans.

The next edict is for Jews to gather their gold and silver and deliver it to the synagogue. Even a family's precious menorah isn't spared. Heirlooms handed down through generations now ultimately belong to Hitler. Everything belongs to Hitler. The Levins don't have silver serving dishes and candlestick holders like some families do, but Eva, Jadzia and Mindla do have gold wedding rings, and Shmuel keeps Chana's wedding ring tucked safely in the bottom of a coffee canister.

With no money, these fine gold bands are the difference between life and death, starvation and survival and there is no way they will willingly hand them to the Germans, even knowing they'll be shot if the rings are found.

One of Jadzia's friends stitches her rings into the arms of a sofa, but Mindla doesn't think this is a very good idea; if the sofa is taken away the rings will be lost, too. A neighbour sews hers inside a tatty old cushion, reasoning that the cushion is too worn to be of any appeal to the Nazis, and she can carry it with her easily if she needs to flee.

Each night Mindla sleeps fully dressed with her shoes on, in case the Germans arrive and she needs to leave quickly. Since her shoes are never taken off she pulls out the lace of the left shoe and hooks the pretty gold band onto it, then carefully threads the lace back inside the shoe with the ring tucked safely out of sight underneath the tongue.

Clever cobbler Shmuel takes Chana's ring out of the coffee canister. He sews a small square of leather inside a boot with Chana's ring safely stitched behind it. To the untrained eye, it looks like the shoe has been patched up, and given his boots are old and worn and of no value to the Nazis, it is the perfect hiding place.

The Germans then snatch furs to line the boots and uniforms of soldiers fighting during the winter months. 'It's not going to stop until they've taken everything,' Jadzia says sadly. 'This is Poland now.'

Mindla is more worried about food than furs she doesn't have. Bakeries are slowly reopening after the chaos of the Seige of Warsaw, but Jews are not allowed to queue for bread. The bread is for Poles and Germans only, and soldiers guard queues to make sure no Jew sneaks in line.

Over bread, loyalty is tested. She thinks of the poor Jewish man betrayed by his own neighbour, who pointed him out to the SS savages and their dogs. The soldiers dragged the man out of the line: 'Ist das wahr? Bist du ein Jude?' *Is this true? Are you a Jew?* they screamed.

When the man nodded, they kicked him to the ground. They repeatedly kicked him in the head, then pushed him into the gutter and shot him. Those in the bread line turned their heads away as if nothing had happened. Side by side they had fought the Germans, but hunger and fear are driving neighbours to betray one another and no-one can be trusted. What savages they've become. Some kind bakers allow Jews to sneak in through the back door and buy a loaf of bread, but they risk their lives doing so.

Mr Landau sets up a communal soup kitchen for the tenants at 17 Muranowska Street. He has come into possession of some food from a warehouse on the outskirts of the city and generously shares it. This is lifesaving for many.

As the weather begins to change and the cooler autumn days turn to winter, the Nazis tighten their grip even further. Jews must provide identification papers upon request, or they will be shot. They are forbidden to work in any government offices, to buy from or sell anything to 'Aryans', forbidden to travel by train or to see an Aryan doctor. Jewish doctors are forbidden from seeing Aryan patients. Yakov keeps his ear to the ground and says there are plans to move all of the Jews in Warsaw into one living area, a ghetto.

Shmuel Levin doesn't believe him. 'Nonsense talk, you'd do better to spend your time finding food than listening to rubbish. This will all be over soon, you'll see; the Allies will come and blow Hitler all the way to Siberia.'

Yakov and Mindla no longer agree with their father, they've lost faith that anyone is coming to rescue them. In hushed tones at home, they begin to discuss the future. Mindla is desperate to be with Kubush. At night, she lies on her bed and waits for sleep to take her away. The same dream comes to her, over and over.

She is reunited with Kubush, living happily in a little cottage somewhere in the countryside. There is no war. She pictures Gad running through wide open fields of lush green grass and skimming pebbles across a little brook. She imagines a small kitchen with sunshine streaming through the window, a jug of milk and a bowl of the juiciest oranges on the table, and little birds chirping at her windowsill.

Dreams are a folly, but they are all she has.

Germans come in the middle of the night and take men away from their beds. No-one knows where they are going or if they'll return.

Just before dawn on a late November morning, trucks pull up outside 9 Nalewki Street, a tenement building just like Mindla's and only a few streets away. All of the men in the building are rounded up and taken away, fifty-three of them.

Day after day their wives and children wait at the Jewish community offices, begging Jewish leaders to help find their men and bring them home. A glimmer of hope comes when the Nazis demand a ransom, thousands of zlotys, for the safe return of these husbands and fathers.

The Judenrat, the Jewish Council, gathers enough and delivers a cheque to the Currency Control Office, but Commander Meisinger refuses to accept it, he wants cash. The next day 102,000 zlotys is delivered. It isn't enough, and they demand another 38,000 zlotys.

The money is a ruse. On 30 November, *Nowy Kurier Warszawski*, the German propaganda newspaper, reports that all the men have been shot, despite the money being handed over. The Nazis refuse to return their bodies, and their place of burial is unknown. It isn't the first time people simply vanish off the streets, never to be seen again.

That same week a new decree is delivered: all Jews must wear armbands to identify themselves, white bands with the blue Star of David. Mindla assumes it makes the task of randomly shooting Jews much easier. 'Papa, we must leave while we can,' she begs.

Shmuel's brother, Uncle Aldo, lives in Sokolka, a village to the northeast of Bialystok and now under Russian command. Mindla believes it is much safer than being in the centre of the Nazis' Polish stronghold.

'I will find Kubush and we can stay with Uncle until the war is over,' she pleads, but Shmuel seems not to hear. As each day worsens, her thoughts of fleeing become more serious.

With winter on its way, she can't imagine how they'll survive with no food and no fuel to keep warm.

In Lodz, southwest of Warsaw, a group of women are seized for labour duties and forced to clean the Nazi headquarters with their bare hands. When the women complain they have no cleaning tools, they are instructed to take off their blouses and use their underclothes. At the end of the day, they are forced to put the clothes back on and wear them, dripping wet and covered in excrement.

Many terrible things are happening all around. Some stories that travel on the grapevine are so ghastly the Levins can't believe they're true. Mindla tries her best to convince her father to flee east but he refuses, leaving her with little option but to go alone. Life in the east will surely be better, she reasons, and there is no time to wait. With Yakov's help she arranges transport on the back of a cart headed to Bialystok. The instructions she receives are clear: just after dawn as the curfew is lifting, she is to be at the corner of Muranowska ready to go.

Everyone gathers around the table that night and Mindla begs Papa to let her take little Shara too. She is six years old and blonde as blonde can be; she easily passes for Mindla's daughter and Gad's big sister.

'We have no food, Papa, there is no school, and Warsaw is no place for a little girl,' Mindla argues. Eva and Jadzia both agree, but Shmuel won't budge. 'She is my daughter; I will care for her. Whatever happens, we will be together.'

Mindla doesn't sleep a wink that night, tossing and turning as a million thoughts race through her head. She is worried about the journey but excited that she will soon see Kubush. Long before sunrise she gives in and gets up. Shmuel is awake too.

'Mindla, I want you to take this,' he says, pressing the treasured gold watch his own father gave him into her hands. 'Give it to Uncle Aldo or use it if you need to.'

'But Papa . . .' she says, wiping away tears.

'No, please don't argue,' he says. He kisses her on the cheek and says goodbye.

Yakov is awake by then too. 'Goodbye, Mindla,' he says, hugging her tight.

With a bag in one hand and her sleepy son on her hip, she gently closes the door behind her and walks away, hoping she will see her family again one day.

CHAPTER THIRTEEN

The horse and cart is waiting in the shadows on Ogrodowa Street, as Yakov promised.

Dawn is breaking over the city and half a dozen or so women are clutching the still-warm hands of their sleepy children who they've dragged from their beds moments earlier. Their husbands cart suitcases stuffed to the brim with worldly possessions. What they can't squash in, they wear; the shirts and jumpers layered thick underneath their coats are a blessing in the frigid morning air.

Mindla worries there are far too many of them to fit in the rickety old droshky, but the driver reassures her he's done this trip many times before and with many more passengers. The women and children will ride in the cart and the men will take turns walking beside. But, the wiry old man warns, they must hurry because the Germans are waking and their patrols will soon begin. If the cart is stopped, the best-case scenario is that the Nazis will steal their belongings, the worst is that they will steal *them*, fresh bodies for their labour gangs.

'We must move,' he says, taking his seat on an old wooden crate.

Quickening their pace, the men strap bags onto the sides of the cart while the mothers and their children pile in and jostle for room.

Mindla squeezes in between two women on a makeshift wooden bench. There is barely room to take a breath, but no-one complains. If she didn't have lice already, she figures she will soon enough. She offers a half smile to the woman beside her, courtesy but nothing more. The children nestle between sacks of oats that will progressively shrink as the driver feeds the old chestnut packhorse tasked with the flight to freedom. The little ones are tired, desperate to lay their heads down again.

'Please hurry,' one woman whispers to her husband as the last of the bags is secured. He taps the wooden cart, signalling to the driver, who flicks a reign to get the horse going. Gently, quietly they roll.

Not so long ago this old oak cart was used for delivering turnips and beets from peasant farmers to the old town markets, but with the bomb-churned fields barren for the winter, human cargo is the driver's only means of income, and business is booming.

The silver-haired man gripping the horse's reigns sits hunched under the weight of his responsibility. He knows that he is carrying more than just these people's most precious possessions, he is also carrying their hopes, their dreams and their lives, any of which can be taken at the whim of an ambitious or temperamental German. He much prefers carting turnips.

Mindla holds her breath all the way along Leszno Street, her heart racing. Her eyes are closed and her ears are pricked for any sound. She dreads the familiar Wehrmacht whistle. She isn't the only one. The woman beside her stares straight ahead, not daring to look around, barely moving a muscle.

When they finally reach the road to Radzymin on the outskirts of Warsaw, a collective breath heaves through the cart and the blood returns to fingers unclenching from fists. The rhythmic rocking and rolling of the droshky as it picks up pace along the country road soothes their anxious souls. When they left their homes this morning, none of the cart's occupants knew if they'd make it past Leszno Street, let alone to Bialystok, but the prospect of life on the other side of the border was worth the chance. Mindla glances over her shoulder, taking in the city skyline one last time. The pink sun rises ahead of her.

Goodbye, Warsaw.

Many hours later, after they pass through grenade-gouged fields, Radzymin appears on the horizon. The picturesque town was home to several thousand Jews before the Nazis arrived. Those who have survived have fled for their lives. It has become an informal checkpoint for the thousands fleeing to the border, so German troops patrol the streets. Technically the border is closed, but the driver says the

Germans have been turning a blind eye in exchange for a little 'tax' for their troubles. Depending on the mood of the soldier, he could wave the droshky through or demand his ransom.

A shiver runs up Mindla's spine as the droshky rounds a bend along the cobblestone street leading in from the outskirts. A sea of olive-green uniforms and coal scuttle helmets greets them. If they aren't in pairs chatting over cigarettes, the soldiers are searching unlucky travellers or stripping the last few shops of their goods, loading whatever they can grab onto waiting trucks.

Mindla and the other women know to keep their heads down, eyes fixed on their feet, careful not to make eye contact, careful not to draw attention. The droshky continues on its way until such time as a whistle or dogs tell them otherwise.

Heads down, rolling, rolling, rolling.

Thankfully it is a busy day for border travel and with many others on the road to freedom, the Germans are kept occupied. This time, the cart is waved on.

On the side of town, the driver picks up the pace and heads for Jadow, where they will spend the night in a farmer's barn, sleeping alongside his pigs. The barn is full of straw and relatively warm, and the smell of muddy pigs makes a pleasant change from the scent of death that lingered in Warsaw.

Mindla finds a little corner for her and Gad to rest. The little boy is happy to stretch his legs and joins the other children running around in dizzying circles at the sight of the pigs. Gad has never seen a pig before and is quite besotted by the littlest swine, who seems to enjoy the children's company too. A black and white one pokes his pink snout through the wooden rails of the pen and the children tickle his nose then run back to their parents. The farmer kindly boils up some of the horse's oats for their own dinner, and with tummies full of porridge, they sleep.

At dawn they set off again, headed for Ostrow Mazowiecka, the next German checkpoint. After occupation, the Nazis ordered the Jews to leave Ostrow Mazowiecka, herding them across the border into occupied territory. The villagers were kicked out of their homes with nothing more than the clothes on their backs. The Germans took possession of their cottages, their clothes, their sofas, their crockery. Everything now belongs to them.

Mindla wonders how any man can rest his head on the pillow of the one he stole from. Those who resisted and refused to leave were brutally executed in a mass shooting a few weeks before Mindla's arrival, but reminders of the dead linger in the town: in the empty classroom where students once sung Hebrew prayers; a family name on a grocery store; a child's bike resting against a garden fence.

This time their luck is out. No-one is passing through Ostrow Mazowiecka today without being searched. As the cart approaches the checkpoint, soldiers wave the driver to the side of the road with their rifles.

'Zejsc!' – *Get off!* – the guard screams in Polish, and blows his whistle.

They line up, men to one side and the women facing them, the children lying low under the benches and sacks of oats in the cart as they'd practised.

'Masz bron?' – *Do you have weapons?* – the soldier barks.

They shake their heads.

'Rozbierz sie' – *Undress* – he yells, pointing his rifle to the ground, where they are to dump their coats and hats. Then one by one they are searched for any sign of hidden valuables.

'Ramiona do gory!' – *Arms up.*

When it comes to Mindla's turn, the soldier begins by patting his way up her legs and around her hips. His hands rub across her stomach. He looks straight into her eyes as his fingers move slowly along the curve of her breasts. She flinches as he squeezes her hard to see if there's anything hidden inside her bra. It takes Mindla every ounce of restraint not to slap him, but she wisely stays still, refusing to even blink, staring straight ahead, slowly breathing in, out, in, out.

He picks up her coat and shakes it, one eye on anything falling, the other on her. Nothing.

Her heart races. *Please don't make me take off my shoes . . .*

Annoyed with his fruitless search, he tosses Mindla's coat on the ground and moves on to the next woman. She is done.

The driver has been watching this unfold from the droshky without saying a word. Casually, he lifts the lid of his wooden bench seat and pulls out a fresh packet of cigarettes. Lighting up the thin roll of precious tobacco, he takes a long, satisfying drag of the cigarette then sits back down. It is the first time Mindla has seen him smoke.

Like dogs to a piece of meat, the smell of the sweet tobacco stops the soldiers in their tracks. The driver offers each of them a cigarette and gives the rest of the packet to the one in charge. They take the bribe and are now more interested in smoking than searching. Another cart comes into view in the distance. By the time they finish their soothing cigarettes, the next cart has reached the checkpoint for inspection, so Mindla's driver is shooed away.

They grab their coats and tumble back into the cart in case the Germans change their minds. As the droshky begins to roll again, the driver smiles to himself. He is a shrewd man and from that moment Mindla feels she is in good hands. She closes her eyes and wiggles her toes. She can feel Papa's gold watch squashed safely inside the tip of her shoe.

The cart trundles towards the border, travelling through muddy farmland, rolling fields and silver-birch forest so thick it shrouds the road in darkness in the middle of the day. At times they pull off into a field and stretch their legs while the horse is fed. The children run around in circles, almost delirious after being cooped up for so long in the cart. Sometimes they are lucky enough to pass an apple tree with a few late-season apples still clinging on. The fruit is nearly always at the top of the tree where others haven't been able to reach. The husband of the woman sitting beside Mindla is nimble enough to climb his way to the top and pick the last of the bounty, which the children devour in minutes.

By dusk the weary travellers arrive at the home of a peasant farmer who will help them cross the Bug river. They are about six kilometres from the Russian border, which lies beyond the Bug. This is as far as the driver takes them, and no sooner has he unloaded their bags than he is gone, heading back to Warsaw to pick up another run of desperate human cargo.

The farmer hurries everyone inside and shuts the door quickly behind them, warning they must remain absolutely silent and out of sight – not a peep from the children. German soldiers regularly patrol the area and they don't take kindly to farmers harbouring refugees. Mindla devours the hot soup and tea the farmer's wife offers; every spoonful of its warmth seeps right through to her cold extremities. The farmer's wife indicates they should lie down and rest. Her kindness reminds Mindla of her own mother. It's been a long time since Mindla has had anyone look after her. She soaks up the woman's strength for the next leg of the journey. In the middle of the night they will walk to the Bug river and cross it, entering the neutral zone between Russia and Germany.

At 3 am the farmer wakes them. Gad is sound asleep, draped over her shoulder. The farmer can see she is juggling a load and Mindla is grateful when he offers to carry her suitcase. Trying not to make a sound, she heads into the inky darkness and follows the others through the fields down to the river bank. It is cold and she can feel the breeze from the river around her legs.

No-one says a word as they shuffle through waist-high grass in the darkness. As promised, a little boat is waiting in the shadows. Without so much as a whimper, the women and children board first and within a few minutes they safely land on the other side, then the boat returns to the shore to collect the men.

The farmer charges two zlotys per person to cross. The business of smuggling people across the border is a well-organised scheme and many people are making money from their flight. The right fixer can mean the difference between life and death. It is known that some wretched swindlers steal the money of innocent people and leave them on the side of the road for dead, but so far Mindla feels lucky. She is so grateful to Yakov for helping her. Their instructions are to follow the road for a few kilometres until they reach the third house. Thankfully they are greeted by a very pleasant old farmer and his wife. For a few zlotys, the man offers shelter in his barn for the night, and will take them by cart to Bialystok tomorrow.

Some of Mindla and Gad's fellow passengers choose to continue walking through the night, but the offer of bread and coffee and a safe place to sleep is too tempting for Mindla and the other women with small children. Every inch of her aching body sleeps well knowing that the next day she will be reunited with Kubush.

CHAPTER FOURTEEN

It is not Kubush but Stalin who welcomes Mindla to Bialystok.

His thick moustache and fatherly eyes smile at her from pictures pinned to doors and windows of cottages in every village she passes through the next morning. Red flags with the golden hammer and sickle flap in the wind. Window boxes are resplendent with flowers fashioned from scraps of red fabric or paper. She is bemused that this strip of land, a heartland of Polish culture only weeks beforehand, is now bursting with Communist pride. She struggles to get used to the sight of friendly soldiers.

The first time she spots the khaki uniform and peaked cap of the Red Army, a chill runs down her spine. Much to her relief, the soldier just smiles and waves the dishevelled hopefuls on in the direction of Bialystok, as does every other soldier they pass.

The black shadow of the Germans disappears with every exhausting step they take towards Bialystok. For the first time in months, Mindla doesn't feel afraid. She is excited; Kubush is here and they will be reunited. She longs to hug him close and sleep with his arms wrapped around her.

Bialystok is a pretty place. Avenues of linden trees, their long branches reaching up to form a tall walkway that heralds the weary women and children into town. The streets are alive with people and soldiers, no-one is cowering or running and there is a sense of orderly chaos.

When they reach the railway station, Mindla bids farewell to her fellow travellers. Their journey together has come to an end. She sees thousands of people camping around the station, hoping for a precious ticket to Moscow or St Petersburg. The trains are scarce and impromptu; there is usually only one a day and those lucky enough to get a ticket in the dawn handout wait ready to move as soon as the carriages reach the platform. Shoulder to shoulder they line up, often from morning until the train arrives later that evening.

Some people have been waiting for days for a ticket, but no-one is angry or agitating; the Russians offer boiled water and bread and people are prepared to be patient. What else can they do? The breezy, almost jovial mood of Bialystok is such a contrast to the fear and foreboding of Warsaw.

The cold-blooded anxiety that has carried Mindla along for the past few weeks is easing, replaced by an overwhelming exhaustion as she allows herself to think that this journey is coming to an end. She just has to find the circus, then she can rest. Gad is tired, constantly grabbing at her arm to be carried, but she simply doesn't have the energy to pick him up.

'We will find Papa soon,' she says, trying to placate him, 'just a little further.'

Bialystok is quite spread out, but she walks towards the town square where she can get her bearings and find the circus. She stops people along the way to get directions. 'Cyrk?' she asks.

More often than not she is met with a puzzled look. These people are newly arrived in Bialystok too; how would they know where the circus would be? Eventually a soldier points her in the right direction.

'Plac Wyzwolenia,' he says, instructing her to go past the Branicki Palace and continue across the Biala river for several blocks. Despite the chill of the winter's morning, her feet burn and a thick cut that has formed where her toes have rubbed against Papa's watch stings painfully. Nevertheless, the thought of seeing Kubush propels her forward. She dusts off her coat and shakes out the woollen bonnet that has kept her warm over the last few days.

She runs her fingers through her hair to try and smooth her unruly curls and neaten herself. It has been days since she's seen a mirror and enjoyed any sort of wash, let alone a bath. Oh, how she longs to soak in a bath of warm, soapy water.

Kubush won't care, she tells herself, he'll be so proud of her when she tells him how horrible things are in Warsaw and how brave she is to have escaped. 'I always knew you were strong, Mindla,' he'll say. Gad is dragging his heels and she lifts him up onto her hip so they can move quicker.

She picks up her suitcase too and marches on triumphantly, heart and hope keeping her going.

Mindla doesn't remember feeling her legs go. Everything turns white and the next thing she knows she's in a kitchen with a woman she's never met. A framed picture of Stalin on the windowsill is the first thing she can focus on. She is confused.

'Drink, child,' the elderly woman says, offering her warm tea, 'you must drink.'

'My boy!' she gasps, suddenly conscious of the strange surroundings.

The woman points to the floor where Gad is sitting on the rug by the fire, happily chewing on a piece of bread. 'You fainted,' the woman explains.

One minute standing, the next gone. The old woman's neighbour carried Mindla inside to her.

'Everything will be fine,' she says, 'you must eat.' She pushes a boiled egg across the little table towards Mindla. Then Mindla begins to remember. She had rounded the corner of Plac Wyzwolenia to see nothing at all. No circus, no tents, no clowns. Just an empty field where the circus once was. At first, she had assumed she had the wrong address. 'Oszuka!' – *fool!* – she cursed to herself under her breath, dumping her suitcase down onto the grass and gently lowering Gad. As Gad skipped through the field, she stopped a man walking by. 'Excuse me, sir, is this

Wyzwolenia?' she asked. He nodded his head enthusiastically, 'Yes, yes, here lady,' pointing to the grassy park under their feet.

'I'm looking for the circus,' she said.

'Odszedl,' he said simply. *Gone.*

Every muscle of Mindla's body shuddered violently. She had come all this way. Her heart was set on finding Kubush today and she wasn't emotionally prepared for any other outcome than being reunited with him. Her legs crumpled beneath her and she slipped to the ground. The kind man carried her across the road to the old woman who lived in an apartment block on the edge of the park.

Now gathering her thoughts, Mindla explains her predicament. The woman explains that the circus was here but has left. Mindla is in the right location, but the circus train limped out about a week ago.

'So sad,' the old woman says, shaking her head, 'the animals are gone.'

As Gad climbs up onto Mindla's knee, weeks of tension come flooding out and tears roll down her cheeks. It is the first time she's cried since her mother died.

Thoughts rush through her mind. Where will she sleep tonight? She has very little money and her father's watch is only to be used in the most desperate circumstances.

The elderly woman brings more tea and gently strokes her hand. From the kitchen window of this apartment, Mindla looks out over the vacant field where her husband was supposed to be.

She shows the woman a little photo of Kubush that she keeps tucked in her suitcase. He is so handsome in his fedora and suit. When she looks at Gad, she swears she is staring into Kubush's big blue eyes.

'Do you have relatives here?' the woman asks. Mindla shakes her head.

'You mustn't sleep on the streets, not with a little one,' she says. 'You can stay here, just for tonight.'

Mindla can sleep in the lounge chair and Gad on the rug in front of the fire. Her husband will be home soon, the woman says, he will understand. She suggests that in the morning Mindla visit the administration building or the synagogue, maybe someone there can help.

Tomorrow, Mindla will begin her journey again.

CHAPTER FIFTEEN

The hypnotic rhythm of the axle's arms clicking over, which had lulled Kubush into sleep, suddenly changes pattern. The circus train is slowly grinding to a halt.

It has been some time since the last wave of applause swept over them, and they've been travelling a long time, but not long enough to be home. Kubush nudges the man on the camp bed next to him and places his finger to his mouth, signalling towards the door.

On his hands and knees, he crawls across the splintered floor, taking full advantage of a gap in the wagon's side panels. It is dark but he can hear Lala.

'My artists are asleep,' she says with faux anger, loud enough to warn them all, but not so loud it is obvious she is doing so, 'this is the very best circus in Europe and we are expected in Warsaw, you are holding up our journey.' Before carefully adding, 'There are no Jews here.'

A deep chill runs through Kubush's blood when moon-light catches the curve of the soldier's black helmet. He

117

silently moves back to his hessian bed, signalling to Faivel, and they both quickly pull out the silver crucifix necklaces they've been wearing tucked under their shirts.

They shut their eyes and lie silent and still in the darkness, feigning sleep.

Jackboots crunch along the gravel. The ladder to the old gypsy boxcar is dropped to the ground.

Kubush thumbs the little chain around his neck and prays to any God that will listen.

Breathe.

The officer pushes through the bright-red checked shirt and overcoat hanging from a makeshift clothesline crudely strung between the walls of the carriage. He shines his torch up and down and around, searching every corner of the wagon for signs of Jewish scum.

On the floor the light catches the bulbous toes of a pair of oversized leather shoes, then inches up to a Bible resting underneath tins of white face paint and talcum powder and a small round mirror on top of an upturned wooden crate, a makeshift dressing table.

The torch slowly follows the line of Kubush's body and when it reaches his shoulders it stops. The tip of the officer's rifle flicks back his blanket, the light catching a glimmer of the small silver crucifix carefully on display around his neck.

Satisfied, he leaves and moves on to the next carriage.

Breathe.

•

Shmuel scurries to the door as quickly as his weary body will carry him. 'I'm coming, I'm coming,' he yells, trying to placate whoever is at the door.

It is early morning and well before curfew, the time of day when only the *uninvited* arrive, and he prays it is not the Nazis.

Shmuel opens the door to find his son-in-law staring back at him. 'Kubush!' Shmuel exclaims, embracing him with gusto. Surprise is mirrored in their eyes.

Shmuel can't believe Kubush is standing before him and Kubush is equally stunned by how much Shmuel has aged in the months since they've seen one another. He can almost feel how brittle the old man's bones are as he squeezes him tight.

Shmuel ushers him inside, quickly eyeing the stairwell to check he hasn't been followed and the neighbours haven't been disturbed by the banging.

'Oh Kubush, I am so pleased to see you,' he says, pulling the kettle onto the stove. 'Sit, sit.'

Kubush notices the old man's hands, once strong from crafting his leather, are now sinewy and knobbled. His once stocky frame is wiry and noticeably hunched over.

'Where is Mindla?' Shmuel asks.

'She's not here?'

Their shoulders slump in unison as they realise this is not good news. There is much to catch up on.

In the quiet of the morning over tea, both men put the pieces of the jigsaw puzzle together. They realise that while

Mindla was making her way to Bialystok via Radzymin, Kubush was heading along the quiet back roads of the eastern regions towards Warsaw. If only she'd stayed put another day or two.

Yakov is the first to join them at the breakfast table. 'Kubush?' he says, rubbing his eyes as if he's seen a ghost.

Yakov has grown so much since Kubush last saw him; he is no longer a boy. He offers his hand as any polite young man would, but Kubush draws him in for a long hug instead and Yakov can hardly contain his joy.

Shmuel cuts a thin slice of bread for Kubush, the last of a lucky half-loaf Mr Landau gave them a few days ago. Kubush can see how difficult life has become for the family. A small bag of kasha is the only thing sitting on the bench under the kitchen window once decorated with colourful bottles of herbs Chana picked and dried from her cousin's garden, with packets of flour and yeast, and sometimes vegetables or fruit lovingly preserved, when she could get them.

Kubush subtly pushes his bread towards Yakov, who has already devoured his meagre half-slice, and nods for him to eat it. He silently resolves to bring them food, confident of the Staniewskis' help.

It is hardly the homecoming Kubush had been longing for. The situation in Warsaw is far worse than he'd imagined and certainly more desperate than Bialystok. The men reassure themselves that by now Mindla and Gad will have found their way to Uncle Aldo in Sokolka, where they will be safe. They agree Mindla is strong and smart; she will be fine.

One by one the family wakes to find Kubush in the kitchen.

A sense of joy surrounds the kitchen table for the first time in months. He tells them about the Nazis invading Bialystok, the bloodshed and heartbreak of losing their beloved circus animals; of burying the lions who died of shock under the deafening squeal of low-flying Luftwaffe; of horses they released into the streets, rather than watch them harm themselves as they thrashed off their reins; of the prized pigs they offered locals for food.

Tears well in his eyes as he describes the human howl of the frightened chimpanzees that still haunts him at night. Lala cradled them like babies in her caravan to try to soothe them.

He tells of how the Soviet army rescued them. 'Mindla and Gad will be safe there,' he reassures them.

Kubush wants to see Warsaw for himself in the morning light. Shmuel gives him the new armband Jews are to wear, with the blue Star of David on display, and for the next few hours Yakov guides him around what's left of the town he loves.

Kubush is shocked by the destruction of Warsaw. The parks and gardens where he and Mindla walked are now muddy fields, chopped up by artillery fire and tanks, littered with trenches and makeshift bunkers left behind by the retreating Poles. But nothing can prepare him for the burnt-out crater that was the great Circus Staniewski. He slumps to the ground trying to take in the stinking debris where animals once roamed and magic happened.

There is no magic today, just tears.

As German soldiers walk towards them, Yakov tugs Kubush's arm to prompt him to get up and follow him quickly, stepping off the street and out of the soldiers' path. Jews are no longer permitted to walk on the street with Germans and must step off into the gutters when one is present. At every corner Kubush sees posters screaming 'Bekanntmachung!' – *Notice!* The headlines list new rules to be observed by Jews.

As they pass various buildings, Yakov points out the horrors that have occurred there, and recounts stories he's heard on the underground grapevine. Stories of soldiers storming into apartments and looting them. Of women locked in rooms with the Nazis, who force them to perform unspeakable acts with a gun at their heads, while their husbands load their precious possessions on to the Nazis' trucks. The Germans justify these 'gynaecological' examinations by the soldiers as being done in case the women have hidden valuables inside themselves.

This pillaging of homes and humans occurs every day.

Nobody knows when or where the Germans will appear next, or how brutally they will behave. Random executions are common. Sometimes six or seven men are shot, sometimes fifteen or more. The scent of death lingers heavily in the air.

Kubush observes people attempting to go about their daily business, but no-one speaks. They scurry, heads down, moving with purpose. Those lined up in queues are frozen figures, their faces forlorn and lowered, not game to make eye contact with anyone. No-one lingers. The joie de vivre of Warsaw's streets is gone. There are no conversations about family or friends, upcoming bar mitzvahs or weddings. There are no street markets. Khaki-clad soldiers hover menacingly in packs, smoking cigarettes, eyes peeled for any opportunity to spill Jewish blood. The streets are soulless and sad, busy with the lifeless fighting to live.

Kubush stays at the Staniewskis' apartment with Faivel and the last of the circus performers who are unable to make their way home. He visits Shmuel and the family as often as he can. With Lala's help, he can bring them some bread and potatoes, a cabbage on a lucky day and sometimes a few handfuls of flour.

He carefully plots different routes through the quiet backstreets, often weaving in and out of damaged buildings or through connecting courtyards to keep off the streets. He visits at different times each day, so as not to draw attention to himself, fully aware a fit and able-bodied young man is ripe pickings for a labour gang. He sees young women with children in their arms and he thinks of Mindla and Gad. In his heart he knows that one day they will be reunited.

CHAPTER SIXTEEN

Uncle Aldo is taken aback when the young woman at his doorstep introduces herself as his niece. She must have been no more than Gad's age when he last saw her and it has been many years since he's seen or spoken to his brother Shmuel.

Still, family is family and he welcomes the pretty stranger and her child into his home and gives them shelter, just as her father said he would. She doesn't plan on staying long, her heart is in Warsaw and she is hopeful of going home. Surely the Allies must arrive soon?

Mindla is grateful of the warm bed to lay their heads on in the meantime. On her first night, Uncle Aldo gives her a cast-iron bucket of water warmed on the stove and some soap, real soap! It is the first time Mindla has washed in weeks.

She slowly unlaces her shoes, careful not to displace the wedding ring tied tightly under the tongue of the right shoe, and eases her battered feet away from the leather. The sharp cold of the stone floor is surprisingly soothing on the blisters and bruises she's almost become accustomed to. She reaches inside the left shoe and pulls out the slip of cotton hiding Papa's gold watch. She will give the watch to Uncle Aldo to help pay her way.

Miraculously, Mindla and Gad are free of lice, but their clothes need some sort of divine intervention. The accumulation of dirt and sweat, the smell of horse and droshky, and the pigs they shared a bed with on the way to Bialystok, have layered the stale stench through every fibre of her woollen dress and coat. It isn't until she strips off her clothes that she realises just how bad she smells. She washes Gad first.

He giggles as the soapy water trickles through his hair and down his back. Over and over again Mindla scoops the water up in the precious blue teacup she's carried with her, and drizzles it over him.

Then slowly she cleans herself with a sponge. The warm water washes over her skin. She notices her arms have thinned and muscle lines are visible around her shoulders, the result of carrying a child in one arm and a suitcase in the other in her journey across Poland.

Uncle Aldo's wife gives Mindla a pair of striped cotton pyjamas, and a shirt of Aldo's for Gad to wear as a nightie. That night she cuddles her little boy into her breast and sleeps soundly, her shoes lined up neatly under her bed. It is good to feel human again.

Given Mindla's skills, the Russians send her to work at Sokolka's tannery. The thick, fetid air of rotting flesh hits

Mindla long before she reaches it each morning. The racks of fresh animal skins hanging up to dry remind her of Mr Landau's factory, although she can't recall it ever smelling this bad. She misses her life before the war. She misses Mr Landau.

Under the watchful eye of Stalin's men, the women work hard. Winter is fast setting in and their soldiers need boots and gloves. Faster, faster. Mindla's job is to make sure the skins are silky smooth, ready for dyeing.

An acid solution, a crude blend of pigeon excrement, salt and lime, strips the animal skins of hair, but never quite removes it all. Over and over again she will force the near-blunt blade across the skin, scraping off the last tufts that haven't come away after their soak in the pungent concoction. Clusters of matted hair shavings curl up at her feet.

The days are long and the stench of the tannery crawls up Mindla's nostrils and clings on. It *never* leaves her. Still, she is grateful to have a job, and thankful that Gad is being looked after by her uncle and aunt.

Sokolka is a pretty place, but cold. Glacial winds from northern Russia are sweeping across the flat farming plains surrounding the town, promising a brutal winter. The tannery is situated on the outskirts in an attempt to keep the smell away from where most people live, close to the train line that runs between Warsaw and St Petersburg. In the few minutes it takes for Mindla to walk there each morning, she imagines how quiet the earthen streets would have been before the war.

Today she steps around people lined up for food at the soup kitchen the Russians have established to feed the displaced masses. Many have slept on the street overnight.

The town is swollen with refugees seeking food and a place to rest. The synagogues and churches are bursting at the seams. Families shelter in every nook and cranny. The grocery stores are slowly opening up again after months of disruption, but their shelves are bare and nothing will grow out in the fields now winter is coming. People are reliant on the Russians to deliver food.

Uncle Aldo has told Mindla of how the Nazis stripped the town bare in the few days they controlled Sokolka. Armed with truncheons and whips they looted homes, businesses and grocery stores like his own, leaving nothing behind. In the middle of the night, the Gestapo trucks ground to a halt along Grodzienska Street. With a pistol to the head, the shops' owners were dragged from their beds and forced to open up their stores and hand *everything* over. By the end of the raid, the Nazis' vehicles were stuffed with the food, clothing and supplies of others. For a handful of days, the little town was crippled with fear. Jews hid in cellars and attics until the Russians arrived to save them, Aldo says. Still, Mindla reasons, at least Sokolka escaped being bombed or burnt down.

•

SUE SMETHURST

The first winter of the war arrives in Warsaw with brutal swiftness. On some days the Levins awake to sky and streets a stark white, the blizzards having blended the horizon with what remains of the broken city. By January, Warsaw is blanketed by thick snow, several metres deep in some places. Many of the occupation's bloodiest secrets are now frozen in time at the bottom of the ice-thick Vistula. Siedlce, east of Warsaw, records days of −41 degrees Celsius.

Kubush hopes that the punishing weather might dampen the activities of the Nazis. He is wrong of course. With their backs warmed by the furs and fuel that belong to hard-working Jews, they forge ahead with gusto. Verboten! – *Forbidden!* the posters scream. Every day a new command. Round-ups are regular: young men, old men, women vanish from the streets. The winter brings new cruelty. Word spreads of a young Jewish man who is singled out on the street and forced to carry slabs of ice in sub-zero conditions. The soldiers insist he work without gloves. His bare skin sticks to the frozen blocks and peels off layer by layer as the day wears on. His hands, bruised and bloodied, have to be amputated.

A group of well-known Jews, including doctors, dentists and lawyers, is arrested by the Gestapo and taken to the Kampinos Forest near the village of Palmiry outside Warsaw. In a glade surrounded by silver birch trees, they are executed and their bodies kicked into huge trenches that become mass graves.

A woman is thrown from a moving tram, and large numbers of Jewish women are seized and taken away for the

Nazis' pleasure. Those lucky enough to survive return home with diseases.

All synagogues and places of worship are closed. Every day a new horror. Food is hard to come by. Fuel even harder. It is impossible to get coal. The faces of those who dare to head out on the street are hollow, hunger etched in their eyes. Children run behind coal carts, scooping up the coal dust as it falls onto the snow. On a lucky day, a chunk of coal might come loose from the load. Some Jews burn books from local libraries to keep warm, while others risk being shot on the spot or arrested for breaking the ever more draconian laws when they sneak out into the nearby forest to collect wood. Still, no-one Kubush speaks with believes this will last. Any day now, the Allies will appear on the horizon.

CHAPTER SEVENTEEN

February 1940

The Bersohn and Bauman Children's Hospital on Sliska Street is due to reopen. It has been shut since the Germans burst in without notice and closed it down six weeks ago, claiming it was infected with typhus. SS guards have been manning the gate since then and only those in a coffin are allowed to leave.

The hospital's director, Dr Anna Braude-Hellerowa, was furious but powerless to do anything about it. 'Of course there is typhus in the hospital,' she argued, 'there is typhus everywhere on the streets of Warsaw!'

The doctors and nurses were forced to sleep on the hospital floor and only a medicinal dose of undiluted spirits once a day staved off the freezing conditions and threat of infection among the patients.

Now that the hospital is reopening, Kubush has suggested to Faivel that the perfect way to celebrate is with a visit from the clown duo of the famous Circus Staniewski. Faivel doesn't hesitate. It will make a welcome change from scavenging for food or hiding from the Gestapo, which have consumed their days.

Kubush and Faivel paint on their brightest smiles in the hope of distracting the kids from their pain. They head into the ward, but Faivel immediately stops as if winded. If there is such a place as hell, he thinks, this must be it. Bulbous eyes full of hope and full of disease stare at them. Kubush doesn't flinch. He stops at the first bed he comes to and offers his hand to a little boy to shake. When the child's skeletal fingers are in his grasp Kubush discreetly moves his free arm, triggering the invisible wire threaded through his coat sleeve. Suddenly, a flap of bright green hair leaps right off the clown's head. The children shriek with laughter.

'Now me, now me,' begs the little boy in the next bed, awakened from his malaise.

Kubush inches along each steel-framed bed and again and again he performs the same trick. The children know exactly what's coming, but still they lap up every moment of his magic. Kubush has missed the joy he feels from masking his face and making people laugh.

Faivel quickly regains his composure and works the opposite side of the long room. 'If beauty were time, you'd be eternity,' he says to one of the nurses in her starched uniform and striped bonnet. He winks as she rushes around the vast ward dealing with a chorus of coughing and the odd blood-stained sheet. She giggles and smiles back at him as he doffs his pretend cap to her.

He takes a coin and waves it in front of a little girl, then tucks it firmly into his palm under her watchful eye. She focuses intently as he passes it from one hand to the other, trying to work out where the prized silver groszy is. After a few sneaky movements and a little circus razzamatazz, Faivel is ready for the grand reveal.

He uncurls one fist – no coin. Then the other – no coin in it either.

He turns his hands over and over again to show the child that the coin has disappeared, then shakes his arms to prove the coin isn't hidden up his sleeve.

'Gdzie to jest?' *Where is it?* the girl quizzes.

'To magia!' *It's magic!* Faivel says, winking. He pats the top pocket of the suit where he'd slipped the coin while she was focused on his hands. A simple but masterful illusion that never fails to delight.

Faivel loves entertaining children. They don't judge him; they don't mock his stumpy legs or flattened forehead. They laugh with him, not at him. He'll walk a little taller knowing he has achieved as much as any doctor or nurse today. There is no centre stage, no lights and no prancing horses at the Bersohn and Bauman Hospital, it is the smallest audience Kubush and Faivel have ever played to, but it is by far the most appreciative.

As they edge along the grey, joyless streets of Warsaw back to the Staniewskis' apartment, the clowns take turns sucking on a prized cigarette. Each long suck of the smooth tobacco fills their noses and throats with something other than the deathly smell of the hospital.

Both men are lost in their own thoughts.

It weighs heavily on Faivel's mind that many of those precious little children won't make it out of Bersohn and Bauman's alive and he makes a silent promise to get back there as soon as he can. Kubush thinks of Gad, and longs to see those big blue eyes that melt his heart.

Mindla feels the change of seasons. The sun, although still weak, is beginning to take the edge off the crisp dawn air as she walks to the tannery each morning. The crust of thick snow that has covered Sokolka's streets is slowly allowing the odd sliver of green grass to triumphantly poke its way through the slush. She steps around mounds of dirty ice, yet to succumb to the spring's warming rays.

The arrival of spring is a relief. The winter has been long and harsh, with Siberian winds pummelling the flat plains around Sokolka. Spring brings a degree of happiness and some feeble hope that the war will soon be over. At the very least, life will be a little easier. As she walks along the dirt road heading out of town, Mindla wonders if the heads of purple crocuses are beginning to appear along the defrosting banks of the Vistula and whether primroses will bloom across the meadows around the town. A carpet of pretty buds would go a long way to transforming the disfigured fields.

Not long after she arrives at the tannery, the workers are called to a meeting. The Soviets have announced a registration. All refugees must decide whether they want to become citizens of the great Soviet state or go home.

It all sounds innocent enough, but that evening Uncle Aldo explains that in fact this is a dreadful game of Russian roulette, trick questions with life or death consequences. The Russians are in fact inviting the refugees to choose between Stalin and Hitler.

Those who stay in the Soviet Union will no longer reside in the border towns and instead be relocated to the gulags of the interior with no guarantees they will be allowed to leave after the war. Mindla may never have another chance to go home, but she knows she is walking straight back into Hitler's merciless arms if she does. If she stays, she must leave the comfort of Uncle Aldo's house and head towards Siberia with no friends or family to help her, to the brutality of a labour camp. It is a dreadful dilemma.

For several weeks Mindla agonises over what to do, conscious the clock is ticking. She tries to put off the decision as long as she can, but when news reaches her that a German refugee committee is on its way, she is forced to decide.

'Mindla, there might be another way,' Uncle Aldo gently suggests. 'If you want to go home, I think I know a man who can help.'

Barely a week later, Mindla peeks through the casement windows beside the cottage door, keeping an eye on the road. Her bag is packed and she has already said her goodbyes. She is headed for the border. It's a risk she knows she must take.

Just after dawn breaks the droshky arrives.

The fixer doesn't say much. He is a young man with an impish face who barely looks older than Yakov. She is sad to say goodbye to Uncle Aldo; he's been so good to her and she is grateful of his kindness and the welcome he and his wife extended to her and Gad. She arrived as a stranger but now feels the warmth of family ties. He hugs her tight and kisses her forehead one last time, as he tucks Shmuel's precious watch into her hands. 'Oh no, Uncle, you must keep this,' she says.

'You'll need it more than me. It may be the only thing that saves you. Be safe, child,' he says with the same look in his eye her father had when she fled Warsaw. For the first time, she sees a resemblance between them.

Mindla doesn't look back. She tucks Gad into a corner of the cart and places her bag under the wooden seat. It barely takes a minute and then they are gone. The fixer explains that it will take most of the day to travel to the border. They'll stop in Bialystok for a rest, then continue westwards. News from the border isn't good, he says, as the Communists and the Germans have placed guards at all crossings. No-one is coming in or out without permission and anyone captured trying to cross is immediately sent to prison, or sometimes shot.

But he reassures her that he knows people and a safe place to cross. They will be fine.

Mindla doesn't ask questions and the fixer doesn't offer much more information. She doesn't know his name and assumes he doesn't know hers. It is better that way.

The wagon quietly meanders along. Other than the odd quibble from a bored Gad, the trip is largely silent and uneventful. By mid-afternoon they've passed through Bialystok, then Czyzew, and as dusk begins to fall, she can see the border village Rostki up ahead. As they approach it, the driver suddenly directs the old horse to turn off onto a narrow road that leads towards thick forest some way off in the distance.

They pass alongside fields, heading towards row after row of ghostly grey silver birches. Their trunks stand to attention like soldiers and cast long shadows as the sun sets behind them. The droshky continues into the heart of the forest and the trees close in around them. When they are surrounded by trees the wagon suddenly stops and the driver indicates it's time to get off.

'Go,' he says, pointing further into the forest. 'The border is just beyond the cutting.'

Mindla squints in the lowering light of dusk. She can just make out a clearing through a thick stand of black alder and ash trees.

'You must hide until well after dark. Russian patrols will come past twice, and after the second patrol you are safe to cross.'

And with a final warning that they must be absolutely silent, for the trees have ears, he begins to roll away. Mindla doesn't wait to gather her bearings, she grabs Gad's hand

and they run into the gathering darkness. After barely a minute, Gad begins to cry. 'Mamo,' he whines; he is hungry and tired.

Mindla scoops him up and continues on until she finds a copse of scrub that offers some shelter. Rocking the boy gently in one arm, she digs into her bag and pulls out a thick crust of bread. He grabs it in his little fingers and sucks on it ravenously as if it's a lollipop. She takes a deep breath as he quietens down. There's no doubt these woods are crawling with spies or soldiers, and she must find a place to hide.

She spots a giant black alder, with thick roots that stretch out across the forest floor, arms open to greet her. The tree is calling her. There is room inside the old hollowed-out trunk to hide so she pushes her back as hard against the tree wall as she can, cuddling Gad in beside her.

She scoops up the remnants of the winter forest floor around them with her hands, and layers the muddy leaves across their legs hoping it will offer some camouflage, then gently strokes Gad's forehead until he falls asleep. In the darkness her mind races.

It is hard to gauge just how far they are from the clearing or how far she will need to run to get to the other side. And what of the other side?

She will need to hide in the forest until she reaches a safe village and can arrange transport back to Warsaw. There is much to consider but she trusts instinct will get them through. First they must cross the border. It isn't long before the inky sky swallows the forest.

Mindla can barely see her hand in front of her. She is hopeful that the moon will give them some light when it's time to head for the crossing. The wait is unbearable.

She's lost track of time but she thinks it has been about an hour since she heard the border dogs make their first sweep. They were off in the distance and didn't come close enough for her to be too worried. In the silence, though, she hears the dogs again, the second patrol.

She listens closely.

The echo of the forest makes it impossible to be sure how close the dogs are. Gad begins to stir as the barking becomes frenzied. A twig snaps from somewhere behind her and she gasps. She quickly grabs a little more bread from her bag for Gad to suck on and cuddles him tight, desperately willing him back to sleep.

Her heart is racing and she holds her breath as she now hears the voice of the guards clearly. They are close enough that Mindla can smell the dogs, so surely they can smell her, smell the bread. *Stupid Mindla*, she silently admonishes herself.

Her face is frozen against the rough wooden trunk and every inch of her body pushes in hard, hoping the tree will magically open up and swallow them inside.

Then a deathly scream pierces the silence and the voice of a guard bellows through the forest: 'Stoj! Stoj!' – *stop now!*

The dogs bark ferociously at their prey. Mindla pities the poor soul in their clutches.

The forest resumes its uneasy silence and Mindla knows they can't stay. The second patrol has passed and as the fixer instructed, she must make her move. She knows this forest is littered with others like her. Will anyone else be brave enough to show their face? She peels herself away from the trunk and dusts the leaves off her and Gad, putting a finger to her lips and then to his to show the little boy he must be absolutely silent.

Slowly she begins to move, clutching Gad's hand tightly. She can barely see a foot in front of her. The clearing is visible with the help of the moon, but as she inches closer her heart sinks. The moonlight illuminates the spiky silver top of a tall razor-wire fence.

Oh, dear God, she thinks, wondering how on earth they will ever make their way over it. There are barely a few metres between the scrub of the forest and the clearing so she inches her way along under the cover of the woodlands, searching for an opening further along the fence.

Then she spots it.

A freshly dug hole underneath the bottom layer of wire, just big enough to take a small adult. Someone else must have made it through here tonight. Within a split second she dashes, dragging Gad with her, and pushes him to the ground and into the hole.

'Crawl, Gad, crawl!' she whispers to the boy, who scrambles through to the other side.

She pushes her bag through after him, then drops face down in the dirt, ready to slide under the wire. It is the last thing she remembers before a rifle butt hits the side of her head.

CHAPTER EIGHTEEN

When Mindla comes to, she finds herself in the back of a truck bouncing across the potholed backroads of the borderlands. Her throbbing head rests on the dirty canvas canopy.

As she tries to swallow she can taste blood at the back of her parched throat. She is dazed, but lucid enough to comprehend Gad is beside her.

'Moje dziecko' – *my baby* – she whispers, moving to hug the frightened child, but she is restrained by a rope tying her hands to a railing behind her.

The eyes of three green-uniformed NKVD officers, Russia's notorious police, are trained on her, intently guarding their human loot. A handful of men have also been captured trying to cross the border tonight, a good night's work for this patrol. At least it's not the Nazis, Mindla thinks.

It is the middle of the night when the truck turns into Kopernika Street and rolls through the giant gates of Bialystok prison. The men are herded off in one direction, while Mindla and Gad are taken into a separate interrogation room, and locked up. A small wooden table and two chairs sit in the middle of the room.

Stalin stares down at them from the stark grey walls, his picture taped beside a thin rectangular mirrored panel from which she is clearly being watched. She begins walking laps of the tiny windowless room, gently bouncing Gad on her hip while patting the little boy's back in a vain attempt to soothe him. He is almost three years old now, no longer a baby, and heavy in her arms. She shifts his weight from hip to hip to take the strain off her back.

After an hour or so it is too much and she curls up on the floor in a corner with Gad on her lap so she can rest a little. It feels good to stretch her legs out and she leans her head against the wall in the hope the thick cold bricks will ease her headache. There's no clock so she can't know for sure, but it feels like they've been cooped up in the little cell for hours. Every now and then she can hear a noise outside: a thump, maybe a scream, guards laughing.

'You are German?' a voice says, startling her awake as the officer abruptly appears, shutting the door behind him and taking a seat at the table. He neatly spreads papers out in front of him across the table.

'Polish,' she replies, settling Gad on the floor so she can take a seat opposite this man.

He looks at Gad closely, studying his blond curls and blue eyes, then looks back at Mindla.

'You are German,' he says. It is not a question. 'What were you doing in the forest?'

Mindla calmly repeats that she is not German, she is Polish, from Warsaw, while explaining how she is trying to get back to her husband, but he quizzes her again and again, repeating the same questions. It's clear he doesn't believe her.

'Who sent you? Gestapo?' he asks. 'And why were you in Sokolka?'

Suddenly Mindla realises her arrest was not random bad luck; she's been set up. Could the fixer have been an informant who had no intention of helping her cross the border safely? He's delivered her straight into their arms. What a fool she was to think she could outsmart the Russians.

She wonders how long they've been watching her, and how much bounty the little bastard gets paid for each lamb he sends to the slaughter.

'I just want to go home to my husband, he is in the circus, Staniewski. Do you know them?' she pleads.

'You are a spy,' he says, abruptly pushing back his chair, 'and Herr Hitler won't be getting you back any time soon.'

He marches out of the room and slams the door behind him. Mindla hears the steel bolt slide across again to lock them in, and she takes a deep breath. Sometime later a woman enters the room. She is older, thickset and wearing a different uniform to the guards. It is Russian but Mindla has no idea what it signifies. A guard is holding the door open.

She walks straight towards Gad, who is sitting on the floor playing, and picks him up.

'I'm sorry,' she whispers to Mindla as she scoops up the child and scurries out.

'Stop!' Mindla screams, 'my baby, wait! My baby.'

The door is locked again behind her and Mindla can hear Gad crying. She begins to cry too. She kicks the steel door with all her might, screaming to the guard to bring her baby back, but it's to no avail. She dissolves to the floor in tears, dry-retching and doubled over in pain.

Eventually, when she's cried herself to the point of exhaustion, the officer who interrogated her comes back. 'Now are you ready to tell me why you were in the forest?' he snaps.

'Where is my baby?' she begs. 'Please bring my baby back.'

'The little German is safe and will be looked after,' he says sternly. 'Who sent you, Gestapo?'

She shakes her head and repeats the story but he isn't satisfied. She pleads with him, trying to reason that she is not a spy. Frustrated, he unlocks the door and directs her to move. He leads her through the narrow passages of the darkened prison. She hopes he's taking her to Gad but instead she arrives at a cell bursting at the seams with women.

'Maybe here you will remember who sent you,' he says as he slides back the steel gate and shoves Mindla inside then bolts it closed again. There must be thirty women in a space no bigger than a little kitchen, their eyes all trained on her. A woman nods to her to sit down and they all shuffle a little closer together to make room for her. Slowly, Mindla begins to take it all in. Thick brick walls, a concrete floor scattered with straw. There is no bed, nowhere to sleep and no chairs to sit on.

The women are squashed together, huddled on the floor, the lucky ones resting their backs against a wall. Their hollow faces are glued to the new arrival. Some stand to try to stretch their legs.

Suddenly the smell catches her. She notices a bucket in the corner of the cell overflowing with excrement. The adrenaline of the last few hours leaves her and she begins to shiver, every muscle twitching furiously. Maybe she is in shock.

Daylight pokes through thick bars covering a tiny window at the top of the wall.

Mindla wonders why they'd bother securing a window so small, as not even a child could squeeze through it.

A different warden comes around with the breakfast rations. The women line up for their meagre offering, a small piece of bread and small enamel cup of coffee. An older woman sitting opposite Mindla signals to her to get up and join the queue. She doesn't feel much like eating but she doesn't know when the next scrap of food might come. Each sip of the bitter coffee burns her throat, which is raw from crying.

In the first week Mindla very quickly learns the rules and routines of the women's block. Because there is so little room, the women can't all lie down at once to sleep. They take turns sleeping. Some stand while others lie down and rest. They sleep in short bursts, a few hours at a time. When it is Mindla's turn she lies there thinking of Gad. She knows

Mindla, Gad and Kubush in Moscow.

Kubush (right, puffing his cheeks out) with fellow clowns from the Circus Staniewski.

Kubush photographed when the circus was touring Krakow before the war; with Faivel; and Lala Staniewska entertaining local dignitaries with Mimi the chimpanzee.

The Circus Staniewski was one of the foremost circuses in the world, famous for its water arena, acrobats and a large collection of performing animals, which toured nationally when not at its permanent home at the corner of Ordynacka and Okolnik streets.

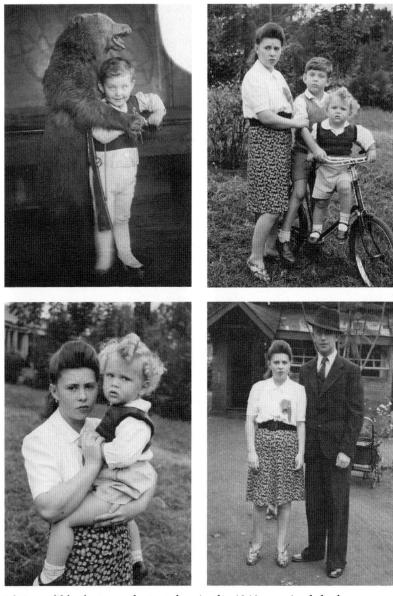

It's incredible that any photos taken in the 1940s survived the long and terrifying journey the Horowitzes made to freedom. *Top left:* Gad hugging a bear at the Moscow Circus in May 1941. *Clockwise from top right:* Mindla at Camp Nyabyeya in Masindi, with Gad and Henry; outside their African home with Kubush; and holding Henry.

Camp Nyabyeya was the improbable Polish village in the heart of Africa where survivors of the war could piece together their shattered lives. Mindla is pictured *(top left)* in her bathers on her way to Lake Albert for a swim, while Faivel *(above)* stands atop a crocodile from the same lake. *Top right:* Gad seated on Faivel's lap next to his mother, with other members of the community. Safe but not yet settled.

The family in St Peter's Square, Rome, on a trip from their refugee accommodation at Cinecittà. *Right:* Mindla's adored sons – Gad, Maks and Henry – before the final passage to Australia.

Top left: Mindla, post war. *Top right:* She never missed an opportunity to get dressed up. She and Kubush made many friends in the Jewish community in Melbourne and enjoyed celebrating bar and bat mitzvahs, weddings and events.

Outside the family home in Moorabbin with Maks and Henry, enjoying the space and security offered by a quarter-acre block in suburban Melbourne.

Jadzia, Samuel and their adored daughter, Hanna, in Germany, March 1949.

Three stooges: Faivel, Kubush and a friend – always the entertainers.

Mindla loved cards. Here she is pictured playing a hand with friends in Melbourne post war, with Faivel by her side and Kubush behind.

Jadzia, Hanna, Kubush and Mindla in Melbourne after the war.

Mindla with her grandsons, Ben (middle) and Ralph in the mid-1970s.

Kubush with his grandson Ralph at Ralph's bar mitzvah, early 1980s.

Kubush hugging grandsons David (left) and Paul.

Kubush in costume ready to entertain as Sloppo the Clown.

Kubush with *Tarax Show* stablemate Norm Brown. Together they performed as Sloppo and Boppo.

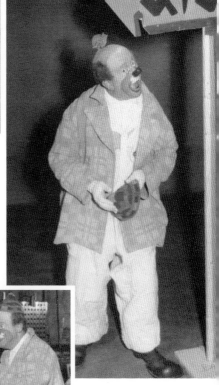

Top: On the set of *The Tarax Show* and *(bottom left)* clowning around behind the scenes. Kubush's trusty jumping flap of hair trick had the Circus Staniewski audience in stitches each night, and clinched him the TV role.

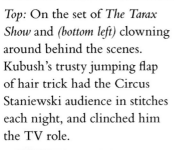

Kubush as Sloppo the Clown in a publicity picture for GTV-9 and *The Tarax Show*.

Mindla, all dressed up and as proud as punch with her grandson, Ralph, at our wedding.

Mindla and Kubush lived for their children, grandchildren and great-grandchildren. Nails always immaculately painted and never without her lipstick and jewellery, Mindla is pictured in these family photos with her great-grandsons, Noah *(top left)* and Jake *(top right)*. *Below:* Celebrating the first birthday of her great-granddaughter, Alexandra, Mindla is with her grandson Ralph (holding Alexandra), son Henry, daughter-in-law Meg and great-grandson Charlie.

he has most likely been taken to a Soviet orphanage nearby. It is some small comfort that he is not locked up in this squalid place.

The women are friendly, but they keep to themselves; trusting no-one is the only rule of survival here. Young and old are snatched off the streets for all manner of random reasons, sometimes no more than on the whim of a suspicious neighbour or a paid informer.

A week after Mindla arrives she is allowed to leave the cell for the first time. She learns that every week or so the prisoners are taken outside to a barren dirt courtyard to stretch their legs. Cell by cell they move in small groups. The women are taken one day, the men the next and so it goes, each cell in isolation so they never mix.

Standing up initially hurts her legs and knees but she quickly relishes being on her feet, walking again, and now she gets to see some more of her new home for the first time. The warden leads them out to the yard, weaving through concrete corridors lined with cell after cell of men, women and some older children, all guests of the NKVD.

Bialystok prison has been designed to hold 1000 prisoners at capacity. Currently there are close to 4000 inmates, and still they come. The prison is receiving dozens of new occupants each day, people randomly taken off the street for so-called offences, some caught trying to cross the border like Mindla, others – particularly academics and intellectuals – on suspicion of treason. The building is bursting at the seams.

All of the cells are the same, located in the basement of the prison. A cold concrete floor and a tiny window right where the wall meets the ceiling that offers just a hint of the outside world. Thinning arms poke through the steel bars as the women walk past.

Mindla tries not to look. She and her cellmates are taken upstairs, bypassing a wing of single cells for prisoners in solitary confinement, and led out into the open courtyard. Guards with rifles cocked patrol the roof, keeping an eagle eye on the women below. Mindla pauses to inhale a welcome lungful of the fresh air, then closes her eyes and rests her back against the brick wall warmed by the weak sun.

'Come,' an older woman warns, 'walk . . . or they'll shoot you.'

A carousel of weary women gently moves around and around in circles for the next hour or so before the barbed-wire gate is opened and they are herded back inside again, back to the dank underground cells. They are fed twice a day, a ration of bread and coffee in the morning and at night a bowl of watery soup and some cabbage, as well as another cup of black coffee. On lucky nights there might be a little porridge too.

Dignity quickly disappears. The women share a galvanised iron bucket for a toilet. Some soil themselves rather than relieve themselves into it, especially when it begins to overflow. The bucket is emptied most days but not always; sometimes it's two or three days before the warden comes.

It's the women's job to carry their shit outside, so they take turns. Whoever empties the spilling bucket gets first use when it is clean.

Every night as she tries to sleep, Mindla thinks of the warmth on her back in the courtyard, and of those glorious few moments of sunshine and fresh air, which carry her through the next week inside. Each day she survives is a day closer to being released, to being with Gad and Kubush, and a day closer to the next time she feels alive again.

CHAPTER NINETEEN

April 1940

Kubush sits on the arm of a plump sofa in the living room of the Staniewskis' apartment, listening intently as Lala reads the newspaper aloud.

'They're planning a ghetto,' she says, taking a long drag of a short cigarette.

She hands the newspaper and the shrinking tobacco to her husband.

Unfazed by the remnants of red lipstick around the tip, Bronislaw draws the last of it hard into his lungs before swiftly lighting another.

'They'll be chased out of their homes,' Bronislaw says, reading between the lines of the *Nowy Kurier Warszawski*.

'Bastards.'

He abruptly tosses the newspaper into the bin and begins pacing around the living room, a trail of smoke and Mimi the chimpanzee following him. The circus master doesn't need to explain the gravity of this news to the faces gathered before him.

A colourful cast of circus characters has called the Staniewskis' apartment home since the outbreak of war. Bronislaw and Lala opened their doors to the orphans of war and somehow provided a bed and a meal for almost a dozen lovable ruffians every night since; clowns, acrobats, trapeze artists, animal trainers and the men who shovel their muck. For some, the circus is the only home they've ever known. And many of them are Jews.

Lala is particularly worried about the Lilliputs; their unusual gait and bulbous foreheads make them an obvious target of the Nazis' cruelty. She is very fond of Faivel in particular, who always makes her laugh, and the darling Weronika Orluk has been with the circus since she was a child. Lala raised her as her own.

'I think I have an idea,' Kubush says.

On the morning of 1 June 1940, Lala lifts up the canvas flaps of the smallest touring tent they own and carefully ties back the sides, ushering the workers in to put the finishing touches to her arena.

Where Mokotowska and Krucza streets meet is a small site compared to the grand locations where the circus has performed in the past. One big-top canvas covers the derelict neighbourhood garden from end to end. One tiny tent squeezed onto the curb facing Mokotowska acts as a box office, while another facing Krucza becomes a dressing room. It is better than nothing.

Dressed in brown jodhpurs and a white cotton shirt, Lala rolls up her sleeves ready for business and directs the men to place the last of the front-row chairs as close to the arena as possible, then sweep away the excess sand from the stage floor.

'These must be the best seats in the house!' she declares. 'Everything *must* be perfect. Our lives depend on it.'

It was Kubush's idea to bring the circus back to life. Surely the best way to save themselves would be to hide in plain sight, to be useful and of value to the Germans, he reasoned. It made his skin crawl to think about entertaining those sadists, but how else would they survive? Bronislaw thought this brilliant, so the circus master donned his finest suit and Lala her most elegant satin dress and silk stockings, and the two of them met the governor of the Warsaw District in early May at his office in the Brühl Palace.

Many a palm was greased along the way to meet with Dr Ludwig Fischer, who required compensation for taking time out of his diary to meet with the charming Polish couple. He was busy with the war effort and the wall he was building across the city to keep the filthy Jews and their diseases away from the Germans.

'Full steam ahead!' he boasted as Lala strained every muscle to maintain the smile masking her disdain as this vulgar man boasted of the establishment of a ghetto.

The baby-faced officer was particularly taken by the voluptuous Mrs Staniewska. He didn't take an eye off the pretty gemstone brooch that sat neatly at the crest of her ample bosom while mulling over the idea of a circus to entertain the bored German soldiers and their girlfriends.

'Perhaps a zloty or two would find its way back to my office?' Fischer suggested. 'A donation to the war effort?'

Bronislaw smiled, oozing charm towards the young man with the piercing stare. 'You are a man who knows business, Governor!'

So it was that permission was granted for the Circus Staniewski to rise from the ashes.

By 7 pm the big top is almost full. Although the sun is lowering in the west, the heat has not gone from the midsummer's day. The circus is surrounded by the government buildings and towering apartment blocks that survived the Luftwaffe. Not a breath of wind will whisper through the narrow streets tonight.

The buzz of the audience taking their seats prompts Kubush and Faivel to sneak a glance around the edge of the red velvet curtain. Kubush's back stiffens. The performers know what to expect – Bronislaw has warned them all – but it is still unsettling to see the entire front row full of khaki uniforms and glass-polished jackboots. 'Where are the hungry lions when we need them?' Faivel says.

Front and centre among the ranks of Warsaw's Nazis is Dr Fischer, who delivered a personal guest list to the

Staniewskis and, with it, a clear warning that he didn't like to be embarrassed. Beside him Kubush recognises SA-Oberführer Ludwig Leist, the town commandant and a close ally of Hans Frank, Hitler's personal lawyer and the Governor-General of Poland. Leist loves a circus and was only too keen to approve the application made by Dr Fischer, believing it would be good for the town's morale.

Bronislaw Staniewski promised a show that would lift the city's war-weary spirits. He is under no illusion of the consequences if he doesn't deliver. He wisely begins entertaining them long before the opening act, when young women in flowing gowns deliver the finest black-market cigars Bronislaw has been able to lay his hands on to each of the Nazi guests while they wait.

The tobacco is a welcome surprise, as is Mimi, who follows behind and dutifully lights each officer's cigar. Fischer roars with laughter as the cheeky chimp begins mimicking him. The hostesses then return with perfumed ostrich feathers and attentively fan the faces of the Germans, who are sweltering in the unusually hot June evening. The Germans are in good spirits, and why not? They have much to celebrate. That afternoon word has reached them that the Luftwaffe has sunk a French destroyer off Dunkirk, in the English Channel. France is within Hitler's reach. Three weeks earlier he'd taken Belgium. Now Norway, Denmark, Austria, Czechoslovakia, the Netherlands, Luxembourg and Belgium are all under the Führer's control. The poison of the German army is flowing through the veins of Europe with unimaginable speed.

Kubush's stomach churns at the thought of making these bloodthirsty beasts laugh. Between them, these men in the front row are responsible for hundreds, maybe thousands, of deaths. It is from their pen that orders come to round up truckloads of Jews and send them to labour camps, or, as would later be discovered, dump their lifeless bodies in pits in the forest.

'At least for tonight they are leaving us alone,' he whispers to Faivel.

Behind the curtain, Kubush and Faivel watch as the gymnasts and trapeze artists go through their final warm-up. They have been rehearsing since Fischer gave approval for the circus to perform. After a year without performing, their circus muscles were stiffened and weak at first, but the rust very quickly disappeared. From dawn until dusk they've been fine-tuning their acts, restoring their suppleness. It feels good to be doing something useful.

But Faivel can't help noticing the thinning limbs of the dwarves who have barely left the Staniewskis' apartment for months, lest they be plucked off the streets or shot on the whim of an officer.

Without the exotic animals to dazzle the audience, and with just a skeleton roster of performers available, the Staniewskis have to be clever with their choreography. Sequins, feathers, smoke and mirrors will help them get by, but even in difficult times Bronislaw doesn't do things by halves, and he has an absolute show stopper up his sleeve.

·

At precisely 7:10 pm a clash of cymbals commands the audience's attention. There's no time for nerves now; it's showtime. Bronislaw smooths the cuffs of his trusty red jacket and straightens his top hat, then strides into the ring bellowing, 'Ladies and gentlemen, welcome to the greatest show on earth . . .'

He takes a bow, and on that cue two ropes drop from sky-high above the arena and a couple of sequin-clad beauties plunge towards the ground, jolted from certain death by a rope twisted around their ankles. The ladies begin twirling in mid-air, their lithe bodies at one with the thin cream-coloured rope propelling an aerial waltz. They are soon joined by a parade of crazy clowns, tumbling acrobats, towering stilt walkers and dogs balancing balls on their noses.

Lala has choreographed a kaleidoscope of colour and movement, a feast for the eyes, to instantly dazzle the audience and capture their attention before the first act is formally introduced. In the absence of big-name performers, she has masterfully focused on physical artistry and captivating displays of great skill. Lighting and music help build tension in the background and create an illusion of grandeur.

In between the main acts of jugglers, contortionists and trapeze artists, Kubush and Faivel must weave their magic. They work harder than ever before and with good reason, because their role tonight is so much more than silly faces and slapstick shenanigans. Lala instructs them to be her eyes and ears. In the precious minutes they are on stage, they must read the audience, note their faces and report back on how the show is faring. While the Nazis laugh, they all live.

Kubush can't help but study the men around the edge of the arena. His big blue eyes search their souls. Dr Fischer doesn't look much older than him, his ruddy cheeks and bulging belly the sign of a man who indulges in all that life has to offer. Ludwig Leist has the slicked-down hair and toothbrush moustache of his beloved Führer. Imitation is the highest form of flattery. Clearly neither of these men worry about where their next meal is coming from.

The circus doesn't normally have an intermission but for tonight only there is a break in between the main acts to give Bronislaw time to prepare the grand finale, and most importantly to allow time for the prettiest members of the troupe to deliver a round of drinks to the thirsty guests.

Bronislaw has procured a few bottles of the finest whisky the black market can offer, a gift for Dr Fischer and his friends for allowing the circus to perform. Of course, it will cost him much more than a nip of spirits: most of the box-office takings for the foreseeable future are to be delivered to Fischer. It is a small price to pay.

As the last few precious seconds of intermission tick down, Bronislaw dusts down his jacket nervously one last time and prepares for the final act. He needs to leave the audience gasping for more. He counts his lucky stars that the Neptune

Divers have been available at short notice. They have earned quite a reputation in Italy and Bronislaw has had his eye on them for some time before the war interrupted his plans. It has cost a pretty penny to bring them up from Italy, not just in travel but in the bribes needed to ensure their safe passage across the border. He hopes they will be worth their weight in gold.

When the curtain rolls back, a huge glass cylinder tank stands in the middle of the arena. Suddenly the spotlights turn to the sky and a diver plunges from above and into the tiny pool. The audience gasps in horror as the diver hits the shallow water then miraculously bounces out of the pool to take a bow.

The trick is to hit the water almost flat, a giant belly flop that spreads the impact over the water. The audience, however, has no interest in how or why; their hands are sore from applauding the feat. The diver leaves the arena and two mermaids take the stage. They descend gracefully into the transparent aquarium, their sequined tails drawing them to the bottom, where they fall asleep.

For three minutes these women don't bat an eye or take a breath. The audience sits in stunned silence, the tension building with each second that passes until the sleeping beauties are 'rescued' by the kiss of a diver after almost five long minutes.

The governor jumps to his feet, prompting a standing ovation from the audience. Whether it is the death-defying act that has excited Dr Fischer, or the sight of the women emerging from the water in sheer costumes clinging to their shapely bodies, it doesn't matter.

Mission accomplished.

The Neptune Divers go on for another ten minutes, the highlight of which involves a woman with her sewing machine stitching together a dress under the water while her husband prepares supper. To the audience, it is like the aquarium doesn't exist. For all intents and purposes they feel like they too are inside an underwater living room, watching the lives of these human fish pass by.

'Enchanting!' shouts the newspaper headline the next day. 'Phenomenal', 'the audience leaves with full satisfaction', 'oh-so opulent', 'a program that will satisfy even the most demanding circus fan'.

With such glowing tributes, the box office of the Staniewskis' circus runs hot and the summer season sells out in a matter of days. Dr Fischer and his bank account are most pleased.

CHAPTER TWENTY

Lice have made a home in the curve of Mindla's ear. She scratches until her skin is raw and blood trickles down her lobes. From head to toe she is crawling, the critters nesting in the warm crevices of her thinning body. The threadbare socks she's worn since she left Warsaw are alive, but she refuses to take them off because they match a pair she knitted for Kubush. Whenever the red wool is close to her skin, she feels Kubush is with her.

Every woman is infested and disease is spreading through the prison. The guards now let them out once a week to wash, and once a day to use the toilet in the hope of stemming the spread of dysentery. It hardly matters when the putrid bucket still ferments in the corner of the cell.

Every few weeks a woman from outside the jail appears with clippers, instructed to shave the prisoners' heads. The men happily submit but the women refuse, knowing it is futile: the lice will fester on their skin and clothes regardless, why lose their precious hair? The hairdresser hacks off as much as Mindla will allow then moves on to the next woman, sympathetic to all who have suffered enough indignity.

The prison is overcrowded and rations are shrinking to feed the new arrivals every day. Each evening, the women receive one cup of what is supposed to be soup, but is actually boiled water with a strip or two of potato skin. On a good day some old animal bones or cabbage may have flavoured the broth, if they are lucky. The bread is black and hard, it tastes like dirt. So does the soup and coffee.

As she sips the meagre rations, Mindla closes her eyes and dreams she is back in Warsaw; tonight she is dining at a restaurant with Kubush. She breaks off tiny pieces of bread and places them in her mouth, chewing each morsel slowly. She imagines she is eating a rich sausage stew. In her dreams the guard hovering over her is in fact a waiter bringing her favourite apple szarlotka cake for dessert. She trawls her mind to recall the delicious tastes and smells of the coffee shops and delicatessens of Leszno Street. Her memories have faded and her senses dulled, but she'll never forget the zest of fresh orange on her tongue or the crunch of a crisp apple straight off the tree. She clings to her thoughts long after she swallows the last of the dishwater soup, the memories filling her heart and mind and strangely satisfying her belly.

Mindla thinks starvation is a cunning plan by the Russians. The prisoners will die or at the very least need the toilet much less. Either outcome makes life easier for the NKVD.

•

Late one evening as the guards come past on the last of their rounds, Mindla calls out through the little window in the cell door. 'Please stop!' she begs, 'I am bleeding.'

There are two men doing tonight's shift. A young man Mindla hasn't seen before unlocks the cell door. He has a pleasant face with fine features and dark eyes that remind her of Yakov.

The ruddy face of his older companion is familiar. Mindla has seen him several times before but doesn't know his name. She is embarrassed because her period has arrived. It is the first time in months her worn-out body has menstruated and a large gush of blood is soaking through her skirt. 'Please can I use the bathroom?' she begs in Polish, explaining why she'd like to clean herself.

The older man squints as if he is in pain, then suddenly lunges at her. He digs his thick fingers into her bony wrist and drags her from the cell into the passage. With the door open and a stunned audience watching on, he slaps Mindla hard across the cheek. She loses her footing due to the force of the blow and tumbles against the concrete wall behind her, hitting her head hard.

'Net pol'sky, suka!' – *No Polish*, *bitch!* he bellows. Stale alcohol spittle lands on her cheeks.

For a few moments she is dazed; her right eye stings and begins to water from the shock. He tosses her like a rag doll back into the cell. The prisoners have been told they can no longer speak English or Polish, only Russian. Mindla didn't consciously break the rules, her Russian is patchy and

160

it just slipped her mind. She scolds herself for making a silly mistake.

The cell door is bolted behind her and for a moment the women sit in silence. Some bow their heads, not wanting to make eye contact, some can't take their eyes off her. Mindla shrinks to the floor. From the back corner of the cell, a woman pulls a large handkerchief she's fashioned from an old tablecloth and passes it along. She nods to Mindla to use it to mop up the blood.

Another unbuttons her shirt and strips down to the cotton singlet she is wearing underneath. She tears a strip of fabric from the bottom of the singlet, then passes it along too. It's only then Mindla notices the frayed hems and torn skirts around her. The other women smile and nod sympathetically, knowingly.

Later the young guard returns and takes her to the prison infirmary. Guilt must have got the better of him. He sits outside while a nurse tends to her swelling face in the make-shift hospital.

Dozens of sick men fill the hospital beds. Of the two closest to Mindla, one is moaning and sweating, his face half-crazed. Mindla can feel his milky eyes on her but she tries not to stare. The other man is stiff and unmoving, maybe he is dead. It's too grim to look beyond them.

'Typhus,' the nurse says, directing Mindla to sit up on a steel surgical bench. 'Hold still,' she says, gently dabbing ointment onto the thick purple bruise that has developed on Mindla's cheek.

'I don't see many women in here, how did you end up in this place?' she asks curiously, introducing herself as Zofia. Her warm Polish accent is comforting and Mindla notices how nice she smells, like Mama's soap. Still, Mindla is wary and trusts no-one. She cautiously repeats the story of her of plight to get home to Kubush, of Gad being taken from her.

'I'm so sorry for you,' Zofia says. She clearly senses Mindla's unease and reassures her she is not NKVD, explaining that many of the prison staff are local residents, Communists or poor people.

Zofia takes a cloth doused in spirits and wipes it around Mindla's hairline and down behind her ears to try to kill the lice and disinfect an infestation that is causing a rash. She'd love to give Mindla a bath but that is not possible.

'I am also a Jew, from Bialystok,' she says quietly as she rummages through a drawer searching for painkillers to soothe Mindla's throbbing head. Her brothers were conscripted into the Polish army before the outbreak of war and she hasn't seen them since. Mindla's pulse begins to race. 'You were here before the war?' she asks. 'Did you see the circus? Staniewski? My husband is in the circus,' she says. Her tongue trips over the words tumbling out of her mouth.

'I know that circus,' Zofia says. 'My neighbour is a performer. A dwarf. Faivel. Do you know him?'

'Yes! Yes! Cheeky bastard!' Mindla shrieks. Her excitement rouses the guard, who pokes his head through the door and snaps at Zofia. 'Potoropis,' – *hurry up.*

Zofia begins slowly sponging the bloodstain off Mindla's skirt, stalling for a few precious moments so they can continue talking. Mindla clasps Zofia's hands and begs her to find Kubush and let him know she is alive.

'I can't promise anything. But I'll try.'

The women have worked out ways to sleep, sometimes nestling their bodies into one another side by side, sometimes lying across one another. On the command of one of the older women, they roll over and change sides to ease muscles stiffening on the concrete floor. Oddly, there is comfort in the touch of another human, even a lice-ridden stranger.

Although they shut their eyes, the darkness offers no rest. All sorts of horrors seep through the prison walls when night descends. In the shadows the women pine for their children and husbands. Harrowing images of war and death, of blood and bombings flood their minds. Mindla has taught herself to block out the muffled sobs. She is sympathetic but she knows she must stay strong to survive; although she misses Gad intensely, she has no room for emotions that may weaken her resolve. No good comes from crying.

Unlike the others, she looks forward to the night-time. It means she has survived one more day in this wretched place and the arrival of dawn means she is one day closer to getting out and being reunited with Gad.

In the dead of night, rats pay a visit. They scurry through the corridors and creep along the women's legs, looking for food or an escape route. They run across faces and gnaw at clothes. Each night the women squeal and furiously beat them away, but Mindla has become quite fond of them and the appearance of these little creatures at dusk brings a smile to her face.

When everything and everyone around them is lifeless, slowly withering inside and out, the rats are alive and energetic. She sometimes saves a crumb or two from the black bread to feed them.

An ear-splitting crack startles Mindla awake long before the sun trickles through the tiny window far above her. The noise is frighteningly familiar: gunshots. For a moment she is disorientated, imagining she is back on the streets of Warsaw, until another shot pierces the silence and the woman lying next to her stirs too, confirming she isn't dreaming.

She lies still, holding her breath, unwilling to move a wasted muscle. Another gunshot rings out. The whip-cracking echo is unmistakable. She counts six – maybe seven – more gunshots in quick succession, then silence. It is impossible to go back to sleep.

Many of the prisoners have heard stories of raids occurring in the dead of night. Guards snatching sleepy prisoners for interrogation, locking them up in isolation for days on end, keeping them in the dark then repeatedly blinding them with a spotlight. Some suspected of spying have been beaten until their bones break, or given electric shocks until they beg for mercy.

But this is a new horror. As the women wake, fleeting glances confirm they have all heard the commotion, but no-one says a word. Later that morning whispers pass through the corridors that a cell was 'cleansed' during the night. With the prison bursting at its razor-wire seams, the guards have begun executions.

During the previous day, men from a cell at the end of the corridor were taken to the garden behind the main prison pavilion and forced to dig a large trench. Afterwards, the men were sent back to their cell for their evening rations, but in the dead of night, guards herded them out into the darkness, lined them up on the edge of the trench and shot each man in the back of the head. One by one they toppled into the mass grave.

The executioners scattered lime over their bodies to quicken the decomposition, but they have not been buried yet. The prisoners assume the trench remains open because there are more victims to come.

Almost immediately, new inmates fill the cursed cell. Mindla wonders if they have any idea what just happened to the men who slept there before them. The mood of the jail now shifts considerably and the women assume they'll die this way too. It's just a matter of when.

In addition to the executions, rumours swirl that guards have begun sending prisoners to Minsk and off to labour camps in Siberia. The women wisely lie low, not wanting to attract attention to themselves. Every time a guard peers through the door an uneasy silence hits the cell.

When cold millet porridge dotted with maggots is served up for their evening ration, they accept it without question, and suddenly no-one complains about the stinking shit bucket. Mindla picks the maggots out of her porridge with her fingers and keeps them aside for the rats.

As more and more prisoners arrive, the routines the longer-serving prisoners have come to know change again. It's been several weeks since the women have left the cell to exercise out in the yard. They only get to wash once every now and then. At dusk one evening when the women should be settling for the night, the warden appears at the cell door. 'Vverkh!' he bellows – *up!* Mindla bristles. It's the old drunk who beat her. The women exchange worried glances, as they've never been taken out at this time of night.

'Vverkh!' he yells again, and they reluctantly file out into the corridor. He herds them through the men's wing, past the cell that has been 'cleansed'. They reach the gates to the exercise yard and with the butt of his rifle he motions for them to hurry up and get outside, locking the gate behind them after the last woman steps out.

The women stand still, huddling together, no-one willing to move. They are fully aware of armed guards watching over them from above. From the watchtower, one fires his gun into the air and the women scatter. 'Pereyekhat!' he screams – *move!*

Slowly they begin to walk, and with each tentative step it becomes clear that they are not being killed today, it is merely their exercise time. For the next hour or so, they wander around the small space in darkness, breathing in the cool night air and stretching their limbs. Mindla counts her blessings that tonight they aren't joining the men rotting in an open grave a few metres away on the other side of the fence. For now.

CHAPTER TWENTY-ONE

Ludwig Fischer is waiting backstage when the curtain comes down on the Staniewskis' evening performance. A sickly feeling washes through the circus troupe as they file back through the red velvet curtain one by one, the spirited applause of the audience still ringing in their ears, to be confronted by the imposing Nazi and his SS bodyguards.

'Dr Fischer,' Lala exclaims, shocked to see him. 'To what do we owe the pleasure?'

'I need to speak with your husband,' he replies sharply, giving no hint of his reasons for visiting. She ushers him into her makeshift dressing room and offers him a comfortable seat alongside a rack of her most beautiful gowns, which he fingers idly. Then she pours him a drink, praying he will be charmed by the intimate surroundings.

Word spreads like wildfire that the circus has uninvited company, suddenly sobering the usual post-show frivolity. Some, like Kubush and Faivel, disappear out of sight. Bronislaw arrives swiftly and greets Fischer warmly. He empties the last of the whisky into a glass for himself, then sits down on Lala's make-up chair, turning himself away from his reflection in the mirror to face the commandant.

'I'm afraid the circus must close,' Fischer says bluntly. 'Highest orders.'

The warm liquor helps wash down the lump in Bronislaw's throat as Fischer explains their last performance will be on 31 July, and they must decamp the next day. They will be allowed two more shows to fulfil existing bookings, Fischer is intent on collecting every last zloty he can.

The directive has come from SA-Oberführer Ludwig Leist on behalf of Governor-General Hans Frank. The two men are close.

'The Führer enjoys the circus,' Fischer says, 'but only German circuses, I'm afraid.'

Before the interruption of war, Hitler used to go to the circus many times, usually with his right-hand man Hermann Göring. Göring always made sure they had front-row seats whenever a show passed by Carinhall, his rambling country estate in a forest outside Berlin.

Hitler particularly loved the trapeze. Oh, how he loved the young women dancing in the air above him, the taut muscles of their athletic bodies contorting almost impossibly, with nothing but a thin metal bar between them and certain death. He found it thrilling to see the provocatively dressed women putting themselves in danger to entertain him. Often, the day after a performance, he would have gifts of flowers and expensive European chocolates sent to them.

There were rules, though, always rules. Jews were forbidden from performing in German circuses, let alone attending them, and Hitler forbade performers of mixed background to take the stage. Black people and those with a disability such as gigantism or dwarfism were banned from the circus.

Now that the Staniewskis' circus has served its use, the people of Warsaw will be entertained by a German circus instead – the famous Circus Busch from Berlin. Houdini used to perform with them and, like the Staniewskis', the Busch troupe has carved a reputation for feats of daring and innovation. The announcement of the Circus Busch has been applauded by the Nazi elite, who will go to great lengths to make sure the season is a success. They even extend the curfew to midnight for those wanting to attend. The admission ticket to the circus serves as a curfew-passport if late revellers are stopped on the street.

Lala and Bronislaw have done a formidable job of pulling together an impressive show in the shadow of war, but the Germans ensure it is nothing compared to Circus Busch, whose grand *chapiteau* rises to even greater heights. The wings of the eagle are soon flapping proudly above the Warsaw skyline. Bigger, better, brighter; the German way, just as Hitler has demanded.

CHAPTER TWENTY-TWO

August 1940

Kubush weaves his way through back alleys towards Muranowska Street, slipping in and out of the shadows and ducking through courtyards as dawn begins to break over the city.

He tiptoes around the sleeping bodies of Jews who have been expelled from Krakow and have flooded the streets of Warsaw, seeking refuge. More and more people arrive each day, skeletons wearing a coat of thin translucent skin, shuffling to find shelter in any available corner. Poor bastards, he thinks to himself.

It's a risk to be out so early in the morning, but not as dangerous as being on the streets during the day, when cocky Nazis are looking for entertainment, and those who still pass as fit young men after so many months of hardship are beaten to a pulp or vanish into thin air.

It is 8 August 1940 and this morning every light post around Muranowska Square is carrying a new Nazi decree.

Kubush glances around and is confident he is not being watched. He snatches one of the posters and shoves it inside his coat as he runs up the wooden stairs of number 17 and knocks at the door.

Shmuel Levin answers. He has been awake since the sky began to turn pink, hoping Kubush would come by.

Kubush smiles reassuringly at the old man as he enters the apartment. He visits as often as he can, bringing morsels of food to supplement the meagre rations the Levins depend on. Reaching inside his coat, he pulls out a little parcel swaddled in newspaper and carefully unwraps it on the kitchen table. There's some sausage, two pickles, a hunk of bread, an onion and some coffee, which should be enough for everyone's breakfast.

Spotting the coffee, Shmuel claps his stringy fingers together with glee. How he has longed for real coffee! 'Thank you, Kubush, we'd be dead without you.'

Through Ludwig Fischer's influence and the thriving black market, the Staniewskis have been able to procure food to keep the circus performers on their feet. Fischer considered it a good investment. Lala always asked for more than she required, knowing leftovers would make their way to those most in need. Bread, bags of oats, horsemeat, some eggs, an apple or two and even a prized kipper had turned up in the Levins' kitchen, and they were truly grateful.

Kubush will never forget how Shmuel's sad eyes sparkled to life, suddenly full of hope, when he unwrapped the whole herring. He leant right over the package, savouring the rich, smoky aroma, making it worth Kubush's anguish while dodging bloodthirsty German shepherds in Nowolipki Street to smuggle the fish across town.

Kubush has grown fond of Shmuel Levin, and despite Shmuel's early misgivings the affection is mutual. Shmuel is a gentle soul who offers his son-in-law the warmth and comfort he misses in his own father. Even when the two men gather around the old weathered kitchen table in silence, their minds burdened by their fate, Shmuel's presence provides a connection to Mindla. At the Levins', he is home.

'Have you heard anything?' Shmuel asks reluctantly, as Kubush takes out the new decree he stuffed inside his coat. He shakes his head, knowing that Shmuel is referring to Mindla, but deliberately diverts the conversation so he doesn't have to think about it. It's too painful.

'It's happening,' Kubush says, passing the bulletin across the table. The crumpled paper announces that all Jews are to live behind the brick barriers their malnourished hands have been building for the past few months. The decree is signed by SA-Oberführer Ludwig Leist.

Shmuel quickly scans its contents, then tosses the poisonous paper into the fire, stoking it until it's reduced to ash, to ensure it leaves no trace whatsoever.

Kubush thinks of the sixteen-year-old girl who was executed for tearing down a similar poster. 'The circus is gone too,' he says quietly. 'Where is everyone?' he asks, suddenly aware of how quiet the apartment is.

'The Judenrat have taken Avraham and Laloshe to work in the labour gangs,' Shmuel explains. 'Each day they leave before dawn to build the ghetto walls. At dusk they arrive home. Every day I see them bruised and beaten. It is horrible.'

Shmuel describes the barbaric conditions in which the men must work. For hours they heave bricks along a human chain until their muscles burn. Neither man dares blink, look the wrong way or show any sign of fatigue or weakness, knowing he'll cop a rifle butt to the side of the head or a bullet through the back of it if he does.

Warsaw has been sectioned off into three areas, one for the Germans, one for Poles and one for Jews. The Jewish quarter – *Judenviertel*, as the Germans call it – includes Warsaw's poorest streets. A rising brick wall surrounds it, which will be topped with broken glass and razor wire.

Avraham and Laloshe know the wall's route intimately and Shmuel is relieved to hear that Muranowska Street forms the northern border, so there is no need for the family to move, at least. They are just a stone's throw from the railway terminal at the end of Muranowska Street that will be used to deliver goods to Jews in the new area, and although no-one says it aloud, it will be a very handy location for smuggling.

None of them can imagine that the cargo loaded at the Umschlagplatz adjacent to the train tracks will be human: tens of thousands of Jews stuffed into cattle cars bound for Treblinka concentration camp.

Jadzia and Avraham's apartment in Podwale Street falls outside the new Jewish zone and they will have to vacate. It is decided they'll come back to Muranowska. Jadzia is sad to say farewell to their pretty apartment on the edge of the old town. She reminisces about summer days taking Siva on walks in her pram along Podwale's cobblestone street, past the towering Barbican that forms the wall of the old town and through the vast gardens around the Raczynski Palace. She used to love resting in the shade of its towering hornbeams. Now she wouldn't dare step foot near its burnt and looted ruins.

Barbed-wire stockades already barricade many streets, stopping the free passage of Jews into other areas of the city. Most Jews are aware of these unofficial boundaries and avoid them to save being attacked. Half a million Jews are expected to live in the new area, an impossible ask when the Jews expelled from Krakow are already camped out on the streets. Shmuel reasons it is probably much safer for them all to be together in one place, shielded from the Germans' attention.

'The wall will protect us,' Shmuel says optimistically to Kubush. 'Keep their evil eyes away from us. We can get on with our lives in peace until this is over.'

On 25 August, the skies over Germany light up as eighty British bombers strike Berlin. Many, like Shmuel Levin, welcome the attacks, believing it marks the beginning of the end of Hitler. 'At last! They come!' he cheers.

Instead, the attack ignites Hitler's resolve. His heart burns for the capital of his glorious Reich, and in retaliation he will move the full weight of the Luftwaffe from tactical air raids of British bases and assets to directly bombing its towns and people. The Blitz will soon begin.

Five days later, on 30 August, a month after the circus closes, a small package arrives at 17 Muranowska. The postman rarely delivers anything to the Levins any more so it is a surprise to find the soft brown paper parcel tucked in the mailbox, addressed to Mr Faivel Ditkowski and postmarked Bialystok.

It is Friday afternoon and although the Levins barely mark Shabbas any more, it was Gad's birthday the day before, so Kubush invites Faivel around for a special meal. Jadzia and Eva have diligently saved enough potatoes and cabbage to make a thick soup.

Shmuel can barely contain himself by the time the two men finally arrive. Grinning madly he thrusts the little package into Faivel's hands. 'What is this, Faivel? A girlfriend?' he teases.

Faivel's eyebrows shoot skywards and his cheeks flush. He is as surprised as the rest of them. He studies Kubush's face, wondering if he is playing a trick on him, and then squeezes the parcel, feeling for clues as to what it might contain. On the back, in a hand he doesn't recognise, it reads 'Zofia. Bialystok.' He doesn't immediately register the name but then the penny drops.

'Zofia is from my neighbourhood,' Faivel points out, his fingers fumbling to unknot the string. He peels back the crisp brown paper to reveal a single red sock. There is no note or letter, no card. Nothing but a red woollen sock.

'That's my sock!' Kubush exclaims, now even more puzzled.

'You speak in tongues, schmuck, you are wearing your socks,' Faivel says, taking a small bottle of vodka he's procured from the pocket of his jacket and then pouring them all a nip.

But as soon as Kubush utters the words, the first clue falls into place. 'This is from Mindla! This matches a sock she knitted for me. It's a message. She is alive.'

They turn the sock inside and out, and check for any further clues, but nothing.

'I'll come with you,' Faivel says, knowing exactly what Kubush is thinking.

CHAPTER TWENTY-THREE

September, 1940

Lala Staniewska tosses and turns. She has been unable to sleep since being told that the circus must close. Having ensured that the final curtain of the Circus Staniewski came down in spectacular style, she is now worried about what will become of her troupe and of her livelihood. Working for the circus has offered the lovable ruffians some protection from the Germans, but without it, she can no longer shield them.

The circus men, young, fit and strong, are ripe fodder for labour gangs, and she fears the worst for her team of female gymnasts. The *Nowy Kurier Warszawski* regularly publishes notices from families looking for missing daughters and sisters, and it is well known that the German brutes pick women off the streets for their pleasure. Lala encourages the performers with international papers to leave posthaste, and she tucks extra zlotys into their final wages to help them escape. But many of her most loyal staff and performers are

Jews. There is only one way she can think to help them, but she must risk her life to do so.

Lala makes her way to Brühl Palace again, this time alone. Bronislaw wants to come, but reluctantly agrees this task is best left to Lala as it will give the impression it's an informal matter and therefore there'll be less reason for suspicion.

The chestnut trees of Saxon Garden are golden and beginning to shed their leaves as she hurries around the park towards Pilsudski Square. A crisp breeze coming up off the Vistula signals another long winter is on its way, but it helps settle the nausea that has plagued her all morning as she contemplated her meeting with Ludwig Fischer, and cools her flushed cheeks.

By the time she arrives at the elaborate wrought-iron gates she is resolute about what must be achieved, although her heart still races as she is ushered along its wide rococo corridors. She knows that behind each wooden door she passes is a Nazi commandant. She feels evil oozing through the thick marble walls.

Her visit to Fischer's office does not call for silk or sequins. She is dressed demurely in a royal-blue skirt that gently drapes over her knee, and a matching jacket nipped neatly under the bust, highlighting her hourglass figure. Inspired by Hollywood star Olivia de Havilland, she has pinned her dark curls back, with two sweeping barrels resting neatly on either shoulder. A handkerchief tucked in her hand mops up the perspiration forming in her palms as she grips an over-sized clutch bag containing an envelope of documents.

It has taken a month, but through Bronislaw's connections and a sizeable payment of zlotys, Lala has obtained false papers for her most loyal performers and staff, and she knows just the man who can stamp them for her.

Entering Ludwig Fischer's office she sees him leaning back in his chair. He looks her up and down admiringly and offers her a seat, immediately launching into a speech about the war effort as if keen to impress her. They chat about the grim tasks of war and Fischer bemoans the change of seasons.

The corners of Lala's mouth quiver as she tries to hold her smile.

By the time they get to the matter of why she is visiting, she slides the envelope across his desk, aware that though he seems quite relaxed, he is ruthless and could turn at any time. She makes sure her hand carefully brushes the top of his fingers as he takes the envelope, watching his face for any sign of wariness. He studies each page carefully.

'And who are these people?' he asks, more out of routine than genuine interest.

'Our most loyal staff, Dr Fischer. We consider them family they've been with us so long. Some since childhood. We've raised them as our own.'

'You are not helping Jews are you, Mrs Staniewska?' he sniggers sarcastically.

'Heaven forbid!' Lala protests. 'Dr Fischer, I can assure you these people will be good workers and loyal to the Führer and the war efforts.'

One page at a time, the ugly swastika is inked in red onto the papers, sealing their validity. She breathes again as she tucks the papers back into the envelope, indulging him in a few more minutes of polite but tiresome conversation before she makes her exit.

But Lala's performance is not over yet. She calmly leaves Brühl Palace and heads home, deliberately stopping at a cafe along the way, in order to check she is not being followed. No rush, no hurry, no panic.

Bronislaw is waiting anxiously for his wife to arrive home. He knows her light footsteps up the stairs, and pours her a drink as he hears her approaching.

'You are brilliant, Mrs Staniewska,' he says, kissing her on the forehead.

That evening, wrapped in her husband's arms, she falls into a deep sleep.

CHAPTER TWENTY-FOUR

Bronislaw ushers Kubush inside the apartment and quickly closes the door behind him, putting a finger to his lips to indicate silence. He presses an ear hard against the wood, listening for footsteps. Lala is by the window, discreetly keeping watch through a slit in the curtain. The smoke from her cigarette drifts above her head. She is deep in thought, her silhouette almost ethereal.

Round-ups and arrests have become intolerably frequent. Every day now a man is taken from his breakfast or dinner table, never to return. Sometimes an entire building or street is stripped of its husbands, brothers and sons, the Germans' cattle trucks transporting them deep inside the Reich to toil in Hitler's factories, or dig trenches at the eastern border in preparation for the attack on Russia. The bodies of those who try to run are left on the street to rot.

In one *aktion*, eleven thousand men and boys are taken in the space of just three days. No-one expects to see any of them again. Actors, doctors, lawyers, academics and entertainers are also the target of the occupying army's attention, and Bronislaw worries he's easy prey now that the circus and its useful bribes are gone. Only time will tell.

After a few minutes of listening closely, he is confident Kubush hasn't been followed, so they get down to business. 'The trunk . . .' Lala nods to Bronislaw.

He lifts the lid off the old box by the dresser in the living room. The flaking paint outline of *Cyrk Staniewskich*, once a brilliant pillar-box red, is still visible on one side of the weathered white wooden panels. He rummages through, tossing an eclectic collection of wigs, posters and costumes onto the floor. Then, using a sharp knife, he edges out a thin panel of wood that fits seamlessly into the base of the box. Only an expert could detect it hides a secret compartment. Bronislaw carefully removes a neatly folded uniform, handing it to Kubush.

'It's perfect,' Kubush says, heaving a sigh of relief. 'I really don't know how I'll ever repay you.'

'Live,' Bronislaw says, drawing his protégé into an embrace, 'just live.'

Kubush studies his face carefully, noting the ringmaster's fine nose and almond-coloured complexion. He is creating a picture in his mind he hopes he will never forget. He does the same with Lala, then kisses her on the cheek.

'Go,' she says, not wanting to dwell on the goodbye.

•

Kubush makes his way back across town to the Levins with the package carefully tucked inside his coat. Faivel is waiting for him at Muranowska Street. Yakov has decided he will join them.

That night, Kubush and Faivel sleep on the floor of the Levins' apartment. Dreams of Gad's floppy blond curls and the trace of Mindla's red lipstick on their baby's cheeks waltz around in Kubush's mind. Long before dawn the three men bid farewell to Shmuel and disappear into the darkness. It's showtime.

Surprisingly, the train is running on time. As it appears on the horizon, Kubush steps out of the shadows dressed head to toe in his railway conductor's uniform and confidently strides to the edge of the platform. 'Excuse me, excuse me,' he says, dipping his cap as he pushes his way through the waiting crowd. Poles aren't allowed to ride in first or second class so he positions himself at the end where the third-class carriage will board, and nods knowingly to the conductor further along the line as the train slowly pulls in to the station.

As instructed, others from the troupe arrived long before dawn too and joined hopeful passengers on the platform, blending into the swelling crowd. Jews are not permitted to travel on trains at all, and there's no guarantee their new papers will suffice if questioned by a real conductor, but it's a risk they're all prepared to take.

'Alle einsteigen,' – *all aboard* – the German voice booms over the loudspeaker, and a whistle echoes across the platform, signalling it's time to leave. Kubush opens the door and passengers clutch their precious tickets to show him as they scramble aboard. He lifts a small child or two and helps the women with their bags and suitcases, amazed that this ruse is actually working. Faivel stands taller in his best suit and hat. He flashes the ticket he purchased with his forged identity card at Kubush and the phoney conductor ushers him into the carriage. Then Yakov does the same, followed by a handful of familiar faces. Riggers, labourers and circus hands who never had a moment in the spotlight but gave their blood and sweat to ensure performers like Kubush did are bidding farewell to Hitler today. Those with new identity papers have purchased tickets for those without.

Kubush hurries the last of the waiting passengers onto the train and when there is no room left, he takes the flag from the pocket beside the door and gives it a wave to signal he is full, then locks the door securely behind him. The whole operation has barely taken three minutes.

He rests his head against the carriage's mahogany wall and takes a deep breath as the platform creeps past him and the train to Bialystok leaves the station. Lala's costume maker has done a fine job of copying the uniform of the Deutsche Reichsbahn. The navy single-breasted jacket design would be easy for a gifted seamstress to stitch: six buttons and a plain turn-up turn-down collar. But only a highly skilled craftsman could embroider the Third Reich emblem with pinpoint accuracy to the sleeve. Only a trained eye would spot the forgery.

Many people risked their lives for this moment and Kubush is profoundly grateful. He pinches himself as he begins his journey to find Mindla and Gad, and on to freedom.

Several days later Lala Staniewska picks up the newspaper and flicks through to find her handiwork in bold print. She reads aloud the death notice: 'Kubus Armondo, famed performer of the Circus Staniewski. Much loved. A service has been held.'

CHAPTER TWENTY-FIVE

Mindla tries to move. Her left elbow is wedged into the ribs of the woman squashed beside her. The same with the woman to her right. All she can do is apologise, as there is nowhere else for her to move.

Her legs are curled up tight to her chest and she rests her chin on them when she is trying to sleep. A woman sits on Mindla's feet, sometimes leaning back onto Mindla's shins when her own muscles can no longer hold her up. Every day more and more inmates arrive. Twenty-four women occupied this concrete hellhole when she first arrived. Now there are almost sixty.

Their bodies are jammed in so tightly it is barely possible to take a proper breath. At times Mindla can feel the thinning air being squeezed from her lungs. Through the tiny window high above them a breeze occasionally finds its way in, but it's tainted with dust kicked up from the passing military trucks and rattling droshkies. She can't remember the last time she was able to breathe fresh air.

Mindla considers herself lucky. Some cells have a hundred people.

The only relief from the overcrowding comes from typhus, when the feverish zombies are taken to the infirmary or for burial. Every day, between thirty and fifty people die in Bialystok jail, but their deaths hardly make a difference. Despite the appalling prison conditions, the NKVD continue their arrests, rounding up teachers, doctors, academics and artists, all accused of being spies or traitors. Some only stay for a night before they are released, others a few weeks. Prisoners are often sentenced for their so-called crimes in their absence – there is no legal process, and with the flick of a pen, a panel of NKVD officers will decide a prisoner's fate. Most are transported to the gulags where they'll remain for anywhere between five and twenty-five years depending on the mood of the officer who sentenced them.

Yard walks have ceased. The women haven't been allowed out of the cells to exercise for several weeks. What Mindla would give for a long stroll in the crisp autumn air. If she dreams hard enough, she can feel the fresh gusts from across the Vistula on her face. She knows the leaves of the linden trees will be turning golden by now.

The clothes the prisoners arrived in have progressively been torn into rags or have worn through. Shoes are such a valuable commodity that the women have been stripped of theirs so they can be sent to Russians in Siberia for the winter. Mindla somehow managed to discreetly retrieve her wedding band from inside the tongue before her shoes were snatched away. She has hidden it in a seam inside her skirt pocket but she knows it will be a miracle if it stays put. Her feet are wrapped in rags torn from the bottom of her skirt, which shrinks every time she has her period, and the remaining precious red sock now lines her bra. Wool is valuable and the sock could be easily snatched off her feet while she slept. She keeps that sock close to her heart.

Daily food rations are reduced to a skerrick of maggot-infested mush and a sniff of coffee.

Zofia has requested that Mindla help as a hospital volunteer. She is tasked with alerting the guards when someone is unwell, then escorting them to the prison hospital. Women regularly faint in the increasingly cramped conditions, much to Mindla's relief.

The hospital ward smells of the living dead, a pungent blend of alcohol antiseptic and slowly decaying bodies. For Mindla it is a pleasant change from the human sewer her cell has become.

She lingers at the infirmary as long as she can, making herself useful by boiling water and washing the clammy faces of the sick. Sometimes she takes piles of the dead's clothes to the laundry and helps boil them to remove the lice. The clothes are then packaged up and sent to the gulags.

One hundred and forty beds make up the prison hospital, and they are always full. The dead are piled up under a sheet or blanket and placed in the corner of the ward until prison volunteers can come and take them away. Mindla forces herself to turn a blind eye to the stiff feet poking out the bottom.

Zofia works long hours, day and night. She barely leaves the prison. Some days she brings Mindla a cigarette or two. Oh, how Mindla loves the feeling of the tobacco on the back of her throat. When Zofia brings her two, she tucks one in her bra to bribe a guard if needed, and shares the other with the women in the cell who have been with her since the beginning. Only a fool would smoke a whole cigarette without sharing.

It was Zofia's idea to send a sock to Faivel. They both knew it was a risk because the Germans inspect every parcel, and wool is scarce. Only a miracle will stop a Nazi from slipping it into his pocket, but it was their only hope of getting a message to Kubush, if he is alive.

Rolls and rolls of razor wire sit atop the fence. The brick wall is at least twenty feet tall, maybe more, and Kubush can feel the eyes of the guard watching him from the turret above.

His eyes follow Kubush's every move along the fence line. The tip of his gun is clearly visible over his shoulder.

'Not even if *I* shot *you* from a canon would you get over,' Faivel jokes.

Number 21 Kopernika Street, Bialystok. The notorious Bialystok prison. It's taken many days, but at last their journey has brought them here.

They arrived in town the day before and went straight to Faivel's family. Just a few houses down was where a girl he knew as Zofia had once lived. 'Yes, Zofia is here,' her mother said when the two knocked on her door, 'but she is working in the prison, always working in the prison,' she says, shaking her head. 'Russian bastards.' It was the final clue they needed. Mindla was in jail.

The next morning, dressed in their most respectable suits and brimming with foolhardy bravado, Kubush and Faivel set off, knowing that one silly move could land them both in jail, too.

Kubush scans the expansive prison boundary for any sign of warmth or welcome, but there is nothing but barbed wire and brick, a cold, heartless exterior. The only entry is a thick wooden door under an intricate wrought–iron canopy, a few metres away from what is clearly the main gate, where trucks bring in the prisoners for processing.

A guard stands to the right, eyes straight ahead, taking no interest in Kubush and Faivel as they sheepishly approach.

'I'm looking for my wife,' Kubush says to the officer, who maintains a stony face and is unwilling to engage.

'Can you help me please? I'm looking for my wife, Mindla,' Kubush says again. The guard just shrugs his shoulders. Kubush is not giving in that quickly; he begins to explain the story of the circus and their separation, how he has come from Warsaw to find her and their baby, oh their little baby, so beautiful.

'She is a good woman and there's been some terrible mistake that she is in jail,' he pleads.

While Kubush begs for help, Faivel discreetly steps away and wanders off around the corner of the prison. Taking in the site, he sees that it has three storeys, but clearly there is a basement level too, with barred windows every few metres apart. Cells.

At the first barred window, he kneels down and peers in.

'Mindla,' Faivel calls out, 'I'm looking for Mindla? Mindla?'

'Zamknij sie' – *shut up* – a deep voice bellows back. Clearly not a cell full of women, but a cell nonetheless. Faivel moves to the next window and gets a similar response.

He can see ten windows along this side of the wall. The windows are small, maybe twenty inches square, too small for even the most petite woman to squeeze through, and the five thick steel bars make the task impossible anyway. Even if they wanted to help Mindla escape, they couldn't. Faivel continues. By the fourth window, he is losing hope but he calls her name again.

'Mindla? I am looking for Mindla? Mindla.'

'She's gone,' a woman yells.

Faivel drops to the ground and presses his face to the bars. 'What do you mean gone?' Faivel demands, 'gone where?' His stomach lurches at the thought that they have missed her; maybe she has already been sent to the gulags. But another voice enters the conversation. 'She has taken someone to the hospital.'

Faivel pokes his thick fingers through the gaps in the bars and drops Mindla's red sock into the cell. 'Please give her this,' he says quickly. 'Tell her Faivel was here.'

•

Kubush and Faivel run to the Employment Bureau as fast as their legs will carry them, and join the swollen queue of hopefuls. The corridor is full of the emaciated and tired, hope carrying their feet a few last steps on the promise of getting a job far away within the great Soviet Union, land of prosperity for all.

They sit and sit, all afternoon. Every now and then the doors of the offices open and the next in line is called. Patience, Kubush reminds himself, we've come this far.

By the time the department shuts for the night he is still no closer to seeing anyone but he is upbeat; after all, he finally knows where Mindla is and someday, somehow, he will free her.

The next morning, Kubush goes back to the Employment Bureau alone. He arrives before dawn and joins the others already lingering outside the building waiting for the staff to arrive.

He queues for several hours and, finally, he is granted an appointment with a Soviet official. Slowly he tells the young woman the story of the circus, about his separation from his wife when the Germans arrived. He argues that there's been some terrible mistake, his wife should not be in jail. And their baby? What of their baby? He begs for them to be reunited so they can begin a life together, working hard for Stalin.

She shuffles some papers and leaves the room. It seems like an eternity before she returns.

'You are a clown, you say? And you were here when the Germans invaded Poland?' She quizzes him cynically.

'Yes. I am prepared to do whatever work is needed. I can do many things, I am fit and strong and I am a hard worker, so is my wife. She is a very good seamstress, and experienced in a tannery,' he says, casting his mind back to the first time they met, when Mindla was on her way home from Mr Landau's factory.

Her face expressionless, the official leaves again, then returns several minutes later with an older man, a man who just happens to have been in the audience of the Circus Staniewski during their shows before the outbreak of war.

Kubush runs all the way back to Faivel's home, barely taking a breath. Grasped tight in his hand are two pieces of paper. As it turns out, the manager clearly recalls seeing the Circus Staniewski. He loved the show and had a wonderful time attending one of the final performances before the Germans arrived. He remembered every act and quizzed Kubush in detail to verify his story. When he was comfortable Kubush was telling the truth and indeed would be a wonderful asset to the Soviet Union, he stamped the documents releasing Mindla from Bialystok prison.

Kubush is instructed to collect his wife from the prison and find his child, then present at the railway station as soon as possible. The Horowitz family are bound for Moscow, where Kubush has been ordered to begin work with the great Moscow Circus.

CHAPTER TWENTY-SIX

The rattle of a bunch of keys breaks the silence and startles Mindla awake.

Her eyes focus on lines of the orangey-pink dawn reflecting off the bars high above her. She assumes the noise means the breakfast trolley is arriving, although it seems a little early today. The thought of the rancid slops makes her stomach churn, but the dirty coffee will be welcome.

When the door swings open there is no trolley, just a lone guard. His eyes scan the cell then land on Mindla. 'Horovitz!' he bellows, 'Vne!' *Out!*

Mindla unpeels herself from the floor as quickly as she can, then navigates through the maze of human legs, every now and then losing her balance, waking a torturously contorted woman trying to sleep.

'Sorry,' she whispers, tiptoeing her way through the bodies. 'I'm so sorry.'

At first, she wonders if Zofia needs her at the infirmary, but instead of heading towards the hospital ward, the guard leads her in the opposite direction, to the processing wing where prisoners are packed onto trucks and sent away to the notorious gulags.

She brushes her hand across her breast, feeling for the cigarette she's hidden away, an emergency bribe if need be. As much as she hates this place, from what she hears it is better than being transported deep into Siberia. A million thoughts swirl in her mind as she approaches the main gate and her hands begin to sweat. Is she about to be sent elsewhere? What about Gad? Where is her baby? What will happen to him if she is taken away? But she dares not speak or ask questions, having learnt the brutal lessons of the past. The guard unlocks a thick steel door and ushers her out. Daylight stuns her eyes and the crisp morning air slaps her face awake.

Instead of arriving in the processing unit, she is outside the prison, standing on Kopernika Street. She wonders where all of the people are, confused about what is happening. Until she sees him.

The tall man takes off his hat and dips his head.

'Kubush! Is that you? Oh, my Kubush!'

She runs to him and throws herself in his arms, realising she is free.

It has been two-and-a-half years since Mindla has seen her husband, and he is even more handsome than she remembers. She steps back to take in every inch of him, running her hand through his hair.

'It really is you!'

'I must look a right mess,' she says, unsuccessfully trying to smooth her stinking, matted hair. It is the first time he has ever seen her without her hair rolled up perfectly, and without her red lipstick. Tears well in his eyes. She is bone-thin, so fragile her cheekbones protrude from her face, but her beautiful dark eyes have not dulled and the spark in her smile instantly reminds him of why he fell in love with her.

He takes off his jacket and drapes it around her shoulders, drawing her frail frame into his chest. Her head nestles under his chin perfectly, just as she remembers, as he squeezes her tight. She draws in a long deep breath. She can hear his heart beat. Through heaving sobs, a tale of heartbreak begins to tumble from her mouth, a waterfall of words cascading forth: of her escape from Warsaw and how she couldn't find Kubush in Bialystok; of Uncle Aldo and the betrayal; of her arrest and that wretched jail.

'But that is all in the past now,' she says, pulling herself together. 'Kubush, we must find Gad today. We must find him today.'

Faivel's mother has bread and coffee – real bread and real coffee – waiting for them when they arrive. Mindla can smell the delicious brew before she walks into the house. She is numb and drunk with happiness all at once. Her fingers tremble trying to clasp the mug.

She savours every sip of Frida Ditkowski's hot coffee. It is the most wonderful thing Mindla has ever tasted, but after two pieces of bread her shrunken stomach is bloated and she feels ill. She stares at Kubush, noting every detail of his face. He has barely changed and she pinches herself that her husband is sitting in front of her, alive.

'I'm hallucinating!' she giggles. 'This is a miracle.'

Frida runs a bath for Mindla and takes her rancid clothes to boil, giving her a fresh set to wear from her own wardrobe until she can rid Mindla's clothes of lice. Mindla is so grateful of the kindness, but she refuses to be separated from her precious red socks no matter how dirty they are. Superstition won't let them out of her sight; they are her good-luck charm.

Kubush says that today they will rest. She needs to gather her strength. The administration office has given him a list of children's homes in Bialystok, and one by one they will knock on every door until they find Gad.

Reluctantly, Mindla agrees that they will begin tomorrow.

'Have you seen Papa?' she asks with some hesitation. Kubush reassures her that the family is alive in Warsaw but he doesn't sugar-coat how difficult things are. 'You know your father, Mindla, he's stubborn and strong. The good news is that Yakov came with us. He has continued on into Russia to find work. He'll probably be in Moscow by now.'

Frida has made a bed for them both and after Mindla has a bath she drifts off to sleep in Kubush's arms. The soft blanket lulls her into a deep slumber. It has been nine months since she has been able to lie down properly to sleep, let alone on a bed, a real bed, with real sheets and blankets. She melts into the cotton cocoon and sleeps through the afternoon and into the night.

When she eventually wakes, she is disorientated and groggy and wonders if she is dreaming. Her fingers reach for Kubush's and they lock together under the sheet. There were so many moments during the long nine months in prison when she'd almost given up hope of ever seeing him again, but here he is, his limbs blissfully entwined with hers.

And today they will find Gad, Mindla promises herself.

Dozens of gaunt little faces greet Mindla and Kubush with suspicion at the House of St Martin orphanage on Koscielna Street. Strangers aren't welcome here and clearly visitors don't come very often. Hollow eyes stare back at the pair, quickly sapping them of the hope that had buoyed them up until their arrival.

There is something about this cavernous baroque building, a coldness that tells Mindla instinctively that Gad isn't here, but even so, she scans every freckle on every little face, up, down and sideways, to be sure.

Kubush speaks with the nun in charge, showing her the picture taken of the three of them before the war. It is Mindla's favourite. Gad is nestled between them in his striped coat and hat, his eyes sparkling for the camera. The nun shakes her head, confirming what Mindla feels in her heart. They will not find Gad here.

In some ways she is relieved, because this is no place for a child. The silence is all-pervasive. In this main room, which backs onto a cathedral, there are thirty, maybe forty children but no noise, no laughter, no giggling, no playing, no songs sung, just a bleak and eerie quiet.

It is the third home they've been to this morning and Stalin greets them at each one, smiling down on the little ones whose dreadful parents were traitors to the mother-land. Papa Stalin doesn't want these potential subversives to contaminate the rest of society.

Mindla knows they must keep moving, but oh how she wants to scoop up every one of these poor little mites and run away with them.

'The next orphanage, that's where we'll find him,' Kubush says confidently.

The last time Mindla walked these streets she was trying to find Kubush. The sense of desperation she feels now is uncomfortably familiar. Today, rich-red leaves line the paths and are slippery under her feet. Sometime soon they will be buried deep in snow.

The children's home at Listopada Street yields no joy. Next on the list is Slonimska Street. By the time they reach it, Mindla's emotions are ragged. She had tried to steel herself for the prospect of not finding Gad, but the rollercoaster of hope and crushing loss she feels each time they walk away from an orphanage chips away at her heart. Tears roll down her cheeks when the house mother at Slonimska shakes her head. Kubush wraps an arm around his wife and kisses her forehead. 'We won't give up,' he says, guiding her out the door.

As they are leaving, one of the nannies discreetly follows them out. They don't notice her until they have turned the corner and she quietly stops them.

'I think you will have some luck here,' she whispers, looking around to check no-one is watching as she tucks a tiny piece of paper into Mindla's hand.

The address is not on the list of orphanages or homes given to them by the administration, and when they stop a passer-by for directions, they find it is just a few blocks from where they are standing. The injection of hope carries them up the hill and around the corner to Wiktorii Street, to a quaint wooden cottage surrounded by a rambling garden.

It is the private home of a Communist Party leader, a charming house with vegetables growing in one corner of the yard. As they open the front gate, they can hear a chorus of little voices singing for Stalin.

A young woman answers the door and reluctantly lets them inside when they explain they are searching for their son. A red flag with the hammer and sickle hangs on the wall of the hallway. She goes to get a tall blonde woman with curls tightly pinned back into a neat bun at the nape of her neck. This woman greets them cheerily enough, and shows them to a room full of children but Mindla senses they are not really welcome.

This is her home, she explains, and she is caring for all of these poor orphans.

Mindla automatically looks for Gad's blond mop of curls, but the children all have their heads shaved. A mother's love is a magnet, though, and she spots Gad sitting on the floor among younger children.

'Gad!' she squeals, instinctively rushing to grab him. She scoops him up in her arms and nestles her face into his stubbly head, but instead of embracing her, he howls, pushing her away.

A knife plunges into her heart as he cries out to the blonde woman, 'Mama.'

Mindla is shocked and totally unprepared for his reaction. During the long and lonely hours in jail she played every second of their reunion in her mind; the joy in his big blue eyes soothed her and carried her through each day. She never imagined he wouldn't recognise her and it shatters her fragile heart to see him clinging to the leg of another woman.

'I am Mama, Gad. It's me, bubba,' she pleads to him, crouching on her bony knees to look into his eyes. She begins to sing the nursery rhymes she soothed him with as a baby in the hope it will jolt him into recognising her.

This ruckus has drawn the attention of the other children, who stop their games to watch. Kubush looks at them properly for the first time, taking in how thin and malnourished they are.

But his eyes are drawn back to his son. Gad is three years old now and so different from when he saw him last. He was just a baby when Kubush went on tour and war broke out. If he can't recognise his mother, how will he possibly know who *he* is? He must not frighten the child. It will take some time for them to rekindle the connection they had, and when the time is right he has some magic up his sleeve. Right now, however, the most important thing is to get him out of this place.

While Mindla tries to soothe Gad, Kubush takes charge of his removal. He shows the woman their picture and the paperwork from the Bialystok administration.

Gad is no orphan and he is definitely theirs, Kubush says, but the woman stiffens her back, reluctant to let him go.

'Such a beautiful boy,' she mutters. 'Our supreme leader Stalin provides amply for them. They are lucky to be with us and not with those who care to destroy the motherland and all she provides. Stalin will bring their happiness.'

Mindla bites her tongue and lifts Gad onto her hip. He is still crying and it pains her to see him confused and distressed, but she is confident he will settle once he is away from this place.

She cuddles him up tight and brings his head to nestle into the nape of her neck. He is older now and much heavier than the baby she remembered, but she virtually skips all the way back to the Ditkowskis' knowing his heart is finally beating beside hers again.

The warmth of Frida's kitchen and Faivel's smiling face remind Mindla of home. She can hardly believe that this day she's long dreamed of has actually arrived, and thanks Faivel for all he has done to get her here. They gather around Frida's kitchen table and she makes Gad bread with honey and pours a cup of tea. Mindla constantly sings the nursery rhymes she sang to him when he was a child, smiling and patting his little hands to try to ease his discomfort at being with these 'strangers'. A flicker in his eyes suggests he recognises something familiar, yet still he refuses to call her Mama, instead saying teten'ka – *aunty*. It pains her, but she knows it will pass, she must be patient. He is here and they are together, and that's all that matters.

That evening as soup and bread are served at the Ditkowskis', Gad bows his head and sings a prayer for Stalin: 'Word of Stalin is with us, Stalin's will is among us, glory to Stalin, three cheers for Stalin.'

From the day Gad arrived at the children's home, he was taught to worship Stalin because everything good in the world was thanks to him. Each day at meal time, the children had to sit at a table in the dining room with their eyes fixed to the kitchen door. Mumma, as the blonde woman insisted the children call her, instructed them to recite a prayer to God for something to eat. The children prayed hard but the door didn't open.

'Now let's see what Stalin can do,' she'd say, urging them to pray much harder, this time to the Soviet leader, not God. They squeezed their eyes tight and pushed their fingers together in prayer. When the door was opened, a trolley laden with food was waiting for them.

'You see, children, God did not answer your prayers, but Stalin did. Stalin gives you what you want. Three cheers for Stalin!'

'Word of Stalin is with us, Stalin's will is among us, glory to Stalin, three cheers for Stalin,' they sang.

As Mindla tucks her son into bed that night, she says her own little prayer, thanking God for reuniting them.

The arrival of morning means it is time to say their goodbyes. Kubush is sad to be farewelling Faivel, but he hopes Faivel will join them in Moscow soon. Faivel lights a cigarette and passes it to Mindla. 'You are too good for this two-bit putz, Mindla.'

Mindla takes a drag and hands the cigarette back before embracing Frida. It has been a long time since she's hugged another woman, and the warmth of Frida's arms makes her feel at home.

'Go well, child,' Frida says.

With Gad firmly on Mindla's hip, she and Kubush set off for the railway station, passing Zofia's house on the way. Even though he is no longer a baby, every few steps Mindla bounces Gad up and down playfully as she used to do when he was little, and he giggles at the familiar game.

When they reach the end of the street, Mindla suddenly stops and hands Gad to Kubush. 'Wait!' she says, running back up the street to Zofia's place.

An older woman whom she assumes is Zofia's mother answers the door and Mindla hands her one of her precious red socks.

'Please give this to Zofia for me,' she says.

CHAPTER TWENTY-SEVEN

November 1940

After two and a half gruelling days rattling across the Russian interior, lunging and lurching along rust-bitten tracks, Mindla and Kubush breathe a sigh of relief when the conductor announces Moscow is ahead.

The temperature inside the steel carriage is near freezing since the old train's heating system broke down just a few hours outside Bialystok. In the absence of blankets or coats, Mindla wrapped Gad in layers of newspaper while Kubush paced up and down the carriage to keep his blood from freezing.

As the train reaches its final destination, the couple catch a glimpse of the spires of Belorussky station. A liaison from the People's Commissariat of Culture, Valery, is waiting on the platform to greet the family and escort them to their accommodation. Kubush is due to begin rehearsals with the Moscow Circus the next morning and it is this man's job to ensure the family settles in comfortably.

Valery's first task is made simple because they have no luggage to collect. The sum of their worldly possessions amounts to the threadbare clothes on their backs and a small leather bag holding Kubush's treasured costume, which he won't let out of his grasp. Valery rushes ahead to his car and holds the door open for Mindla, bowing his head to her as she steps into the shiny vehicle.

'It is a great privilege to have a performer from such a renowned circus on Soviet soil,' he says politely. Mindla is bemused by his enthusiasm and wonders if he has any idea that she's spent the last nine months covered in lice and smelling of excrement.

He chauffeurs them through busy streets, reeling off a checklist of things he will attend to for them: tomorrow he will take 'Mr Kubush' to the circus, then he will take 'Mrs Mindla' shopping. Mindla and Kubush are quickly learning that artists and entertainers are highly regarded by Stalin and his comrades, on par with Communist officials.

'Everything will be taken care of,' Valery says. 'But,' he adds apologetically, 'cooperative accommodation is very hard to come by and although your names have been placed on a waiting list it may be a little while before an apartment becomes available. If you don't mind, you will stay at a hotel until then.'

'That will be fine,' Mindla says, assuming it will be something austere and small, 'as long as we have a place to rest our heads.' All she wants is a hot bath and a warm bed.

She is immediately struck by how clean and cosmopolitan Moscow is. The Warsaw they left was a city of rubble and ruins, but this place is untouched by war. It is everything she ever imagined, with its grand buildings and gilded onion domes, and reminds her of how pretty her hometown was before Hitler arrived.

They cross the Moskva River and enter Red Square, travelling past the high red walls of the Kremlin, and then the marble mausoleum holding Lenin's sarcophagus, before pulling up in front of the Hotel Moskva, in the heart of the city. Red Square and the Kremlin sit to the hotel's left and the world-famous Bolshoi Theatre to its right.

'Here we are,' Valery says, taking off his brown houndstooth cap.

Neither of them dares speak, but Mindla shoots Kubush a glance that barely disguises her excitement. The modern Hotel Moskva stands out like a beacon against the traditional Russian architecture. Eight imposing stone columns welcome guests into a majestic six-storey building. The lobby alone is a feast for the eyes and Mindla doesn't know where to look first. Her eyes run up and down the towering drapes and her mind races, imagining all of the dresses she could make out of the rich gold-and-red silk that cascades to the floor. She's never seen such beautiful embroidery. Plump upholstery, intricate mosaics and more lavish fabric decorate every inch. She tilts her head up to take in colourful frescoes that adorn the ceiling.

This hotel was built in the Baroque style as a tribute to

Stalin – on the orders of Stalin himself. It is a home away from home for officials of the Supreme Soviet governments, the Communist Party elite and the Russian bourgeoisie who want to rub shoulders with them.

Mindla's thoughts are interrupted by the dramatic chords coming from a piano off to her left, and she realises it's been such a long time since she's heard music. A clique of military officials lounges around sipping vodka, deep in conversation, oblivious to the pianist's fingers waltzing across the glossy keys. Only a couple of weeks ago, Mindla was locked in a filthy subterranean vault, but here she is, surrounded by such opulence. She soaks it all in, savouring every moment. The mood is so relaxed and buoyant she momentarily forgets about Hitler marching his way across Europe. Maybe the Russians have, too.

She suddenly becomes very aware of her raggedy skirt and feels embarrassed. The scarf covering her hair while she travelled now makes her feel like a peasant. She lifts Gad up and manoeuvres the little boy to drape his arms around her shoulders to hide her stained blouse. Thankfully, their room is ready and Valery returns to escort them up to the fourth floor.

As he opens the door Mindla stops dead in her tracks. She swallows hard to stop herself squealing. The apartment opens to sweeping views across the city, and the entrance salon alone is bigger than the cell she cowered in for nine months. Thick Afghan carpets decorate the floor, a lavishly upholstered sofa rests against a wall, and heavy silk drapes frame the windows, through which she sees a horizon of gold, the gilded spires of St Basil's Cathedral and the Great Kremlin Palace. The Ivan the Great Bell Tower is so close she could reach out and touch it. The Kremlin's red walls pop against a stunning canvas. There is nothing drab or small about this apartment.

'Thank you, Valery, this will be most suitable,' Kubush says with graceful understatement, giving a sly wink to Mindla, who can barely contain her excitement. Valery nods, then dons his cap as he reminds them he will return tomorrow morning at 6 am sharp.

'Three cheers to Stalin!' he says.

When the door is closed and Valery long gone, Kubush ruffles Gad's hair and then scoops Mindla up in his arms and twirls her around. 'I promised you when we married that I'd treat you like a princess, didn't I! Well, Mrs Horowitz, three cheers to Stalin!' he jokes.

A weak sun tries to break through the dark skies as Valery and Kubush head along Tsvetnoy Boulevard to the State Circus theatre. For hundreds of years, the circus has been a fixture of Russian life and Kubush is pinching himself to have been given such an opportunity. At first glance the arena is much smaller than his beloved Circus Staniewski in Warsaw; it has a domed roof around two storeys high and offers shades of grandeur and Soviet ambition, but it doesn't compare to Bronislaw's skyscraping arena. Still, it's not the size of the arena but the magic that happens in it that matters, Kubush thinks.

In the arena, Valery introduces Kubush to his trainer and choreographer Mikhail Rumyantsev, known all over Europe as Karandash. Kubush dips his hat to the elfin man standing before him. Karandash is Russia's premier clown, adored, loved, feted by the Russian people. 'I will be learning from the very best,' Kubush tells him. 'I am truly humbled.'

Karandash was one of the first graduates of the state circus school in 1930 and made his name imitating Charlie Chaplin, but more recently and to the delight of Stalin, he has perfected mimicking Hitler. Every evening he paints a sharp, black toothbrush moustache under his pointy nose and tumbles and trips across the arena, mimicking the Nazi goosestep. He makes the Führer look a bumbling fool and the audience, particularly the Central Administration of State Circuses, can't get enough of it.

The Russians take the art of the circus very seriously and the clown is the beating heart of every performance. When Karandash isn't performing or rehearsing, he trains young protégés in the subtleties of mime and physical trickery, and with sixty-nine State Circus troupes performing all over the Soviet Union, he is kept busy.

Karandash doesn't need fancy props or wild animals to entertain. His costume is a simple blue suit and checked shirt with a matching blue felt fez. His make-up is nothing more than a thick line of black kohl dragged under his dark eyes, and two exaggerated arches above. No white paint, no bold lips, no red nose. It is Karandash's smile and his twinkling eyes that make the magic: a cheeky wink, a telling nod, a raised eyebrow at just the right time, and the audience is eating out of his hands.

'Make me laugh,' Karandash says to Kubush, testing his skills.

Kubush steps behind the main curtain and changes into his costume. When he comes back out onto the arena, he walks up to Karandash and shakes his hand. Immediately his faithful old hat comes to life, flinging a flap of red hair high off his head. Karandash nods approvingly. 'Nice, nice.'

'Now without,' he says, pointing to the props.

Kubush strips down to just a shirt and pants. He walks towards Karandash with his arm outstretched to shake again, but just as Karandash offers his hand in return, Kubush's rubbery legs twist and contort until it looks like his limbs are melting onto the floor. He wavers, then springs back upright, stiff as a plank of wood.

'Good, good, very clever,' says Karandash, impressed that the young man is capable of performing both *belyi* and *ryzhii* personas of clown: the white clown and the red clown, or the elegant and the disorderly.

Kubush is hired on the spot and paired up with another young clown, also new to the State Circus, and together they learn routines and in particular their roles as bumbling German soldiers to Karandash's Hitler. At first, Kubush's circus limbs are stiff, but it doesn't take long for the suppleness required onstage to come back, and in no time he is tumbling and twisting like a teenager. They will rehearse for a few days then begin performing the following week.

While Kubush is busy learning the ropes of the Moscow Circus, Valery is helping Mindla get settled. He takes her to a tailor who measures her up for skirts and blouses and a much-needed winter coat. She chooses polka-dot silk for an evening dress to wear to the circus. Gad will have a coat and shirt and some new pants. The tailor suggests blue striped flannel for a winter shirt for Gad. The clothes will be delivered to the hotel the following day.

Now at least they have pyjamas, coats, sweaters and gloves for the winter. Mindla would happily set fire to the clothes she's worn across Poland, but she will pack them away and keep them just in case.

Valery arranges for a Russian language teacher to begin classes with them immediately, and an instructor in the Communist Party doctrine has been assigned to the family, too. There is much to learn but Gad is well ahead already as he chatters away to Valery in Russian, who bursts with pride when the little boy sings for Stalin.

'Solnyshku!' *My sunshine!* Valery claps.

Mindla often thinks of home. It feels indulgent and strange to have food on her table and clean clothes in her wardrobe. She's never seen this sort of luxury and at times it makes her feel uncomfortable and guilty, but she knows that Papa would be happy for her and relieved she is being well cared for. Though she misses her brothers and sisters terribly, it is probably for the best that she doesn't hear any news from Warsaw. The Germans have issued a decree forbidding Jews from leaving Poland. The borders are now officially closed to Jews, and worse, all Jews living in Warsaw must move into a designated area, the ghetto.

CHAPTER TWENTY-EIGHT

Mindla pulls back the curtains to find the Moscow skyline gone. Its harlequin colours have become a blank canvas of winter-white snow.

The second winter of the war is forecast to be more brutal than the first. The frigid weather dampens Mindla's appetite to explore her new surroundings. She can cope with the cutting winds from the Baltic, but the stinging tail of a northerly barrelling down off the Barents could freeze an elephant's heart. On those days it is painful to be outside and common sense says there is little reward in leaving the hotel. She never gets bored in the apartment. She makes up for lost time with Gad, losing herself in the small, blissful moments of motherhood she craved when she was in jail. There is always someone coming to visit. In fact, she's hardly ever alone.

Each morning the language teacher comes, followed by the commissary for her culture lessons after lunch. She is picking up the Russian language quite well, but learning to write it is much harder.

Valery comes each day as well, but she never knows when he will arrive. He pops in now and then, bringing little parcels of bread or cheese, sometimes coffee or butter, and checks if there is anything she needs.

'You are making good progress, I hear,' Valery says while bouncing Gad up and down on his knee, 'and you are making acquaintances.'

Mindla flinches, wondering if he's referring to the young woman who lives in the apartment opposite. Mindla bumped into her and she introduced herself as Helena.

'You are new here,' Helena had said, not so much a question as a statement.

Mindla had gestured to the exquisite fur draped around the young woman's thin shoulders. 'What a beautiful coat.'

They chatted for a few moments about fashion and the weather, small talk. As it turned out, Helena's husband was a musician with the Bolshoi Orchestra who kept similar hours to Kubush.

'Would you like to join us for a drink sometime?' she asked. By us, Mindla learnt she meant a small community of artists, singers, pianists and entertainers of various descriptions who also called the Hotel Moskva home. Most nights, a motley crew gathered in the lobby for a nightcap when they returned from their shows.

'Of course!' Mindla enthused. 'We'll join you tonight after Kubush's performance.'

That evening Mindla makes an extra effort to get ready, fussing around in front of the mirror to make sure there isn't a hair out of place. She carefully rolls her hair and pins it back off her forehead just as Jadzia and Eva taught her, and just as she'd worn it the very first time Kubush took her to the circus.

Up close she is quite pleased with her appearance. She hasn't aged too much despite the challenges of the last few years. She is thinner, yes, but the deathly bag of bones Kubush rescued from prison is womanly again, even her wilted breasts returning to their youthful shape thanks to Stalin's generosity.

She pouts at her reflection, then dabs one last dot of the brilliant red lipstick that Valery had got for her onto the bow of her lips. Turning her head from side to side, she checks every angle. Her creamy skin has come to life with a swipe of pillar-box red.

With one last look at herself in the mirror, Mindla takes Gad's hand and they head to the circus. From the front row of the auditorium, Mindla and Gad have a perfect view of the evening's performance. Mindla was eager to see Kubush perform but he insisted on waiting a few days until he was settled into his routine and had shaken off the circus cobwebs.

He has no reason to be nervous. For two hours the audience barely sit still in their seats. Mindla adores the dancing bears, particularly an enormous brown one who is twice the size of his handler but nevertheless somehow balances his towering frame on a tiny tin roller, then rides a child's scooter. So clever!

Gad wriggles in his seat when a glossy black seal rolls his doughy body out onto the arena then climbs up a small set of stairs onto a podium where he juggles balls on his nose. The seal's trainer tosses balls high up into the air, which the seal catches on the tip of his nose, then flicks into the crowd for the audience to catch.

But the highlight of the show is Kubush. It has been so long since Mindla has seen him on stage she's almost forgotten how clever he is, and Gad has never seen his daddy performing. 'Da!' he squeals as Kubush tumbles his way into the spotlight.

Karandash is also given a rapturous reception. He receives a lengthy standing ovation when he takes his final bow. What the Moscow Circus lacks in glitz and glamour, it makes up for in heart. This is the people's circus, and the audience is made up of those whose hands work hardest for the Communist cause. Karandash tugs at their heartstrings because he pays homage to the working man and pillories the bourgeoisie.

At the end of the show, as they are about to leave, the plump woman who has been sitting next to Mindla begins to thumb her pretty polka-dot dress.

'How much?' she asks.

'For my dress?' Mindla says, puzzled. 'It's not for sale.'

The woman shrugs her shoulders. 'Pity,' she says, walking away.

Mindla wonders why, if the woman likes her dress so much, she doesn't buy one of her own. After all, hasn't the Communist state provided for everyone as it has for Mindla and her family?

On the way back to the hotel they pass a group of people gathering outside a shop. It is snowing and almost eleven o'clock and the shop is obviously closed. Mindla later learns the shop is a bakery and people begin lining up overnight to get their bread. By daylight, all of the bread will be gone. Maybe Stalin's benevolence still has some people to reach, she muses.

When they arrive back at the hotel, Mindla takes Gad upstairs and tucks him into bed, then joins Kubush and their new acquaintances in the lobby for a nightcap. The crowd toast Stalin, curse Hitler and sip vodka.

Once the toasts have ended, Mindla turns to Helena and tells her about the strange woman at the circus.

'It's because they cannot buy clothing of their own,' Helena whispers. 'Never sell your clothes; you will not be able to buy any more.'

Over vodka, Mindla and Kubush learn that some of the artists have been living at the hotel for many years while waiting for accommodation. No-one is unhappy with the arrangement, because the hotel gives them more than the standard few square metres per person the government allocates. Fully furnished.

'Do you plan to go home?' Mindla asks Helena.

'We are all home now, Mindla. Russia is our home,' Helena says, smiling awkwardly.

'Of course,' Mindla replies, quickly correcting herself.

Later as they are walking back to their apartments, Helena takes Mindla's arm and leans in to her. 'Be very careful,

Mindla,' she whispers. 'The walls have ears and the sky has eyes.'

'I hear Mr Kubush is performing very well, very popular,' Valery says, unwrapping a little container of coffee.

'You are so kind to us, Valery,' Mindla replies, no longer blind to his generosity and fully aware of the stakes of this dangerous game. She wonders who he really is and which agency he works for. Is he NKVD? Valery is not his real name, she feels sure, but that's what she'll continue to call him. And she will smile and be grateful and play along. She wonders if they will ever be free.

During their daily lessons, Mindla sings for Stalin with gusto, the good little comrade. If loyalty to Stalin is what it takes to survive, then Mindla's blood will run deep Russian red.

She and Kubush have heard the rumour that many thousands of Poles who fled the Germans and found refuge in Russia have been sent to the gulags. Their crime was hope; choosing to hold on to their Polish papers to return home when the war ended instead of accepting the Soviet papers as Mindla and Kubush did. They wonder if this has happened to Yakov. No-one has seen him since he left Bialystok on the train with Kubush, promising him he would meet up with them in Russia.

Mindla worries about him, and thinks of her sisters often. Sometimes she refuses to eat her own food because this helps ease her guilt, giving it to Kubush and Gad instead. Kubush, however, reminds her that at any time, at the whim of Valery or one of his comrades, their food supply could stop. She must eat and she must be grateful for what she has. Starving herself in Moscow will not change the situation eight hundred miles away.

'The best thing we can do for the family is live,' he tells her.

New Year is a time of great celebration for the Russians and not even the constant news of war dampens the Muscovites' spirits as 1940 comes to an end.

Mindla and Kubush are invited to Helena's apartment for Russian champagne. Before midnight they make their way out to Red Square, joining thousands of revellers gathered to hear the Kremlin's bells ring in the new year. With the first deep tintinnabulations of the brass, Kubush takes his wife in his arms and kisses her passionately.

'Happy New Year, my darling,' he says, resting his chin on her head, 'whoever imagined we would find ourselves here!'

Moscow has been good to Mindla and Kubush, better than they could have ever imagined. So good, in fact, they have discussed whether they might permanently make it their home when the war finally ends. But they realise after several weeks of learning how things work in the Soviet

Union that there isn't a choice. No-one leaves here of their own volition.

As the vibration of the bells comes to an end, the soldiers guarding Lenin's tomb begin their majestic changing of the guard ceremony. The only sound that can be heard across the snow-lined square is the snap of their leather boots marching in unison.

'Let's go home,' Mindla says, a chill running up her spine.

CHAPTER TWENTY-NINE

22 June 1941

Mindla cannot sleep. It is just before dawn and Kubush is already awake.

He offers his cigarette and she slowly draws the menthol into her lungs, hoping it might help lift the fog from the sleepless night. Mindla hands back the cigarette and wanders over to the window, opening the curtains. It is the coolest part of the day and she savours watching the pink sun rise over the city as she sips her coffee, knowing she'll have to close the curtains again soon to keep the apartment from sweltering. She ponders taking Gad to the cinema to escape the heat while Kubush is rehearsing.

She pads into the kitchen and flicks on the radio while she prepares Kubush's breakfast. It is the usual Sunday broadcast of calisthenics. As she stands in the kitchen scrambling eggs, she stretches a leg desultorily, promising herself she'll do more exercises later in the day.

•

Around 10 am Mindla leads Gad out of the hotel for a walk to get some bread before the heat of the day sets in. Red Square is bustling with couples enjoying coffee or a leisurely breakfast, or reading the papers.

Mindla doesn't care too much for sport but the local football team, Dinamo, lost the USSR football championships yesterday and the newspapers are filled with reports lamenting the embarrassing result. It is big news in the cafes of Moscow and broadcast through the loudspeakers in Red Square.

There is no inkling that the Germans are on their way until 11 am, when the voice of Soviet Foreign Minister Vyacheslav Molotov interrupts the sports broadcast.

'Today at four o'clock, without declaring any demands towards the Soviet Union, without a declaration of war, the German army attacked our country,' he says, in a solemn voice that stops the nation in its tracks. 'This unspeakable attack on our country is a treachery. The Soviet people will deal a death blow to the aggressor.'

Mindla is almost at the front of the bakery queue but bread is now the last thing on her mind as she grabs Gad's hand and races back to the apartment, running as fast as she can with him in tow. She turns on the radio and twists the dial furiously until she can pick up an international station. Despite the crackle, there is no mistaking what she is hearing.

The Wehrmacht is flowing over the border. Stuka bombers are howling over Russia. German boats are anchored in rivers.

Tanks, trucks, bikes and thousands of soldiers on foot clog Russian roads.

Mindla's body reacts dramatically to the news. Her legs turn to jelly and she slowly slides down the kitchen cupboard to the floor. Her chest is tight and she struggles for breath. In an instant she is back in Warsaw and the piercing whistle of the bombs is alive in her ears. Where are the bomb shelters here? Where will they hide?

The ashtray fills as she smokes one cigarette after the other. When Kubush walks in the door late that evening, he finds his wife sitting on the edge of the sofa, suitcases piled up around her. Despite the heat, she is dressed in her coat and hat, ready to leave.

'We must run, Kubush, tonight, while we can,' she insists, the fear written all over her face.

'Don't worry, Mindla,' Kubush says, as he gently takes off her hat and places it beside him. 'Stalin will unleash hell on Hitler. By tomorrow he'll have blown the Germans back to Berlin.' He sits down beside her and attempts to wrap his wife in a hug, but she shrugs him off.

'How can you be so sure?' she asks.

'You should have seen the circus this evening. It was full to the brim and no-one seemed in any way panicked. In fact, quite the contrary. There is a sense of confidence in the air. Karandash stepped up his insults to Hitler and at the end of the performance the audience stood to a rousing rendition of the Soviet national anthem.'

'Only fools underestimate that man,' Mindla pleads. 'I have seen his might. I have felt his fury, Kubush.'

'Look,' Kubush says, pointing to the Kremlin, which, unusually, is still lit up. 'Stalin is there right now planning how he will crush those German bastards. You'll see.'

The following morning, Kubush is preparing to head off to rehearsals when a knock at the door startles them. Mindla's stomach drops when Valery walks in.

'Good morning, comrades,' he says, head bowed and hand on heart. 'Ah, here he is! My favourite little Bolshevik!' He grins and ruffles Gad's blond curls.

He kisses Mindla on the cheek and wanders to the window. 'Such a beautiful home,' he says, looking out at the view over the city. 'Stalin looks after us well, does he not?'

'It is good to see you, Valery,' Kubush says, ignoring the not-so-subtle reminder that at any time Valery has the power to toss them out onto the street. He pats the man's back like he is greeting an old friend. It's been some weeks since they've seen Valery, and Kubush assumes he is visiting less frequently because they've proven their loyalty to Stalin. Mindla is more sceptical; she suspects he is kept busy spying on others whose allegiance may be in question.

'Kubush, these are challenging times,' Valery says, getting straight to the point. 'But the Party is well advanced and our success is assured. Hitler will be on his knees very soon, I promise you. The morale of our people at this time has never been more important, Kubush, and our father has great plans for you,' he continues.

It turns out that rather than closing the circus as Mindla and Kubush feared, Stalin is in fact expanding its reach. New troupes will be formed to head to the front line and entertain the soldiers, and ensembles shipped off to towns and villages around the Soviet Union to lift the spirits of the war-weary Russian people. Along with their regular performances, which are essential to the morale of Muscovites, Kubush will also be required to help train new recruits in the art of clowning. The State needs everyone to do a little extra at this time.

'I'd be honoured,' Kubush says. 'Long live Stalin!'

Once Valery has gone, the two of them sink down on the sofa and sit in silence, not quite sure what to make of this news.

'If Valery is so confident that victory is on the horizon, why will they need circus troupes to head to the front line?' Mindla whispers. Kubush agrees. Valery's great news is in fact a dire warning that the Kremlin is preparing for a long and brutal battle ahead, and the circus is tasked with masking the grim reality of war.

In the days immediately following the German invasion, the news broadcasts all but confirm Mindla and Kubush's gut feeling that all is not going to plan. Molotov calls for volunteers to dig trenches around Moscow, and help construct foxholes, bomb shelters, bunkers and anti-aircraft posts. Mindla bristles at the sight of Muscovites digging up the city's gardens, for it is horrifyingly familiar.

Yet each night at the Moscow Circus it is business as usual, just as Stalin instructs. The clowns, acrobats and magicians do their bit for the war effort by spreading propaganda and reassuring the audience it has nothing to fear.

Karandash is in his element mocking Hitler. 'Our art needs to be raised to battle!' he declares to his charges during rehearsal, ensuring he too plays his patriotic part. In a new routine, Karandash enters the arena carrying a briefcase, which he sets down beside a lectern. A little dog hops out and climbs up onto it, propping up his paws as if giving a speech. Without prompting, the dog begins to bark into the microphone.

Karandash takes him down, but the dog jumps right back up again. This goes on several times, the adorable mutt barking and barking until Karandash yells, 'Stop blathering!' Eventually the dog finishes his 'speech' and climbs back into the briefcase.

Karandash then delivers his punchline: 'The speech by Minister of Propaganda, Goebbels, is finished.' The audience roars with laughter.

Karandash's mockery almost brings the house down, until 'Hitler' trots out into the arena, a pig with a large belly, flabby bottom and stick legs. The audience erupts, united in derision. Insulting Nazis is good for national morale.

On 3 July, Moscow comes to a standstill.

'Vnimaniye! Vnimaniye!' – *attention!* – a voice bellows through the loudspeakers. 'Listen to the speech of the chairman of the State Committee of Defence, Comrade Stalin!'

Mindla suddenly stops smoothing the bedsheets and hurries to the kitchen so she can listen properly. 'Sshh, Gad darling,' she says to the little boy playing noisily in the living room. 'This is important.'

It is the first time Stalin has spoken publicly since the outbreak of war and you can hear every breath as the father of the Soviet Union takes his place at the microphone, pours himself a glass of something then begins his address.

'Comrades! Citizens! Brothers and sisters!' he bellows, 'despite the heroic resistance of the Red Army, the enemy continues to crawl forward.'

Mindla's palms begin to sweat and a rush of heat surges through her body as Stalin reveals that Lithuania has fallen to the Nazis, along with a large part of Latvia, the western region of Byelorussia and part of the Ukraine. Key cities like Murmansk, Smolensk, Kiev and Odessa have been heavily bombed. Crawling forward? Hitler is sprinting.

'The motherland is facing grave danger,' he continues. 'The treacherous Germans are continuing their attacks and I turn to you, my friends.'

He calls for volunteers to join the Red Army, imploring citizens rich and poor to defend 'every last inch of Soviet land and be ready to fight with every last drop of blood. There is no place for whingers or deserters, or panic mongers.'

•

Some flee, but on the whole his pleas work. Almost immediately, people rush to volunteer and long queues form at the army hospital outside Moscow as people wait patiently for hours to donate blood.

Kubush and his colleagues work around the clock for months. During the day they teach willing conscripts the art of circus, then at night they do their best to ignore the signs of war and deliver the morale-boosting magic Stalin requires of them. If a clown chasing a loose swine with a swastika on his back around the arena aids the war effort, then they are happy to oblige.

CHAPTER THIRTY

October 1941

Kubush's head has barely hit the pillow when a knock at the door startles him. He checks his watch. It is 2 am. The rapping continues, confirming he's not dreaming.

He moves as fast as he can, but the noise becomes louder; someone wants his attention urgently.

'Stalin is leaving,' Helena says, the words tumbling out of her mouth. 'An armoured train is waiting for him at the station. It's time to go.'

Mindla had been in such a deep sleep she hadn't heard Kubush arrive home or felt his warm body slipping into their bed, but she is wide awake now and Helena's news jettisons any trace of sleepiness.

Over the past few days, word has filtered through that the Germans have surrounded the town of Vyazma on the outskirts of Moscow. Half a million of the Red Army's best soldiers are trapped behind an impenetrable ring of Panzer tanks.

And yesterday, rumours spread through the hotel that Germans were spotted in the city. Some shop owners opened their doors and told locals to take whatever they needed, rather than surrender their goods to the Nazis.

Helena says that Kremlin guards are lining the platform as the train waits in readiness to evacuate the Leader at any time. His closest staff and advisers are waiting aboard. The gravity of Stalin's evacuation hits them.

'They say Lenin's embalmed body has already been removed,' she adds. No tsarist jewels or Hermitage treasure mean more to Russian people than the sarcophagus of their spiritual leader, and even in death, where Lenin goes, his people follow. Helena paces up and down in front of the window and peaks through the curtains every so often, as if she will see the Gestapo marching through the thick fog blanketing the city tonight.

Mindla doesn't need Helena's news to tell her the Germans are getting closer. She can feel it viscerally. It's the same chill that crept across her skin as the Germans rolled into Warsaw. She's been preparing for this moment for several weeks, squirrelling away extra food, hiding it in a cavity in the apartment roof in case Valery or his colleagues pay one of their random visits. Thankfully there is no chance of that now. If Stalin is evacuating, his most loyal lieutenants will be right behind him. It is every man for himself.

•

The city is eerily quiet when Mindla and Kubush creep out of the hotel barely an hour later. There is not a soul to be seen. Gad is cuddled up, his head resting on Kubush's shoulder, sleepy and oblivious to the panic. Mindla made him porridge before they left, and even though he was too tired to want to eat she shovelled spoonful after spoonful into his mouth, not knowing when their next meal might be.

The Kremlin is in complete darkness, shrouded in the soupy fog, and the colourful domes of St Basil's are camouflaged by a layer of snow, conditions making it virtually impossible for the Luftwaffe to attack the city.

Neither Kubush nor Mindla have second thoughts about leaving. Moscow is a prized scalp for Hitler and he'll show no mercy to her occupants when he arrives. As they reach the metro station, they suddenly realise why the streets are so empty. There is barely standing room on the underground platform. Hundreds are sheltering from expected bombs, others have their worldly possessions slung over their backs, bound for destinations beyond the Volga river in the south or the Ural Mountains out east, hoping the terrain will be impossible for the Wehrmacht to cover.

The next train is due to depart at 5 am. Lord knows how they will all fit on it, but there's no way any of these people will be left behind. Mindla and Kubush decide to head for Totskoye, where the Polish army has been allowed to set up a base.

At exactly 5:10 am, with lights off and windows blackened to obscure their position, the stealth train rolls out of the station and into the inky darkness. Each carriage and the old wooden cattle cars following are full to the brim, but no-one makes a sound.

The journey east is painfully slow. During the day they inch forward, seeking the cover of Russia's thick forests whenever the Luftwaffe arrive. Sometimes they are stuck waiting for hours until the German bombers retreat and it is safe to move again. Passing through open fields, they are sitting ducks. At night the train snakes through the mountains in total darkness, with lights off and windows shrouded in coats or clothes or whatever can be found to camouflage them. Mindla wonders how the train driver can see any more than a few feet in front of him.

There is no food or water available on the train, but whenever they stop, ever resourceful, the evacuees quickly pile off the train and stuff handfuls of ice into their mouths, or fill empty food cans and containers with snow.

Three days later, the train, swollen with wilting human cargo, limps into Totskoye station. It is only then the passengers learn that at the last minute, Stalin decided to stay in Moscow and fight, believing his presence would boost the morale of the battered Red Army. Some are buoyed by the news, while others fear that his death – and Hitler's victory – are only a matter of weeks away.

•

The tiny village of Totskoye offers a demoralising hint of what is to come. The Horowitzes arrive to find there is no accommodation and the railway station provides the only shelter from punishing winter winds. The small platform is jam-packed with people standing up after the long journey or sitting on layers of newspaper to stop their skin sticking to the frozen ground. A handful even fall asleep.

Food is even more scarce than Mindla imagined. They have ample water from the knee-deep snow around them, but the daily food ration promised by the army is little more than weak tea and a piece of stale bread. It is horribly familiar. Thank goodness she has some of her own supplies stashed away, but she knows she must ration them very carefully.

She gives her portions of oats to Gad to stave off his hunger. She has a few slivers of cheese, too, which are rock-hard, but her little boy gobbles them up ravenously nonetheless. What's left of the dwindling morsels she carefully wraps up and hides inside a bag that never leaves her sight. Heaven help anyone who dares attempt to steal a precious crumb.

At the same time, thousands of Polish prisoners of war have been released from the gulags after an amnesty is reached between the exiled Polish government and the Soviet Union. The intention is for these men to now serve in a Polish army alongside the very government that jailed them, led by General Wladyslaw Anders. But there is very little food and shelter for the Anders army, let alone the thousands fleeing Moscow who join them.

They hastily erect makeshift tents, and the cattle cars attached to the train are uncoupled so they can be used for accommodation. Each cattle car can sleep about forty people but there are thousands in need of shelter, and Mindla, Kubush and Gad share their draughty wooden cattle car with sixty or so others. Sometimes more, sometimes less as people die from starvation and the sub-zero conditions, or move on to a new town to try their luck. Sanitation is a trench at the back of the wagon. Lice quickly return and Mindla knows typhus will follow.

At night, the three of them squash into a rudimentary bed for one inside the wooden cattle car; in contrast to the tents of the poor souls outside, it is luxurious, but Mindla never sleeps. In the darkness, she hears the dull thud of bombs hitting the earth somewhere far off in the distance. She's not sure if it's real or a persistent nightmare, but it plagues her mind and robs her of sleep nonetheless.

Her only comfort is the deep howl of a wolf that echoes around the tundra. She hears it at the same time every night and finds beauty in the animal's fierce cry. She imagines it is a she-wolf, a mother calling out to protect her pups. It is strangely comforting to know they are not alone on the frozen fields of the Russian interior.

The Anders army is recruiting to build their ranks, and Kubush, still fit and strong from the circus, decides to enlist. He lines up with hundreds of men, young and old, Poles who have been in Soviet prison camps, stick-thin men with barely a layer of leathery flesh left on their bones, a rifle thicker than the arms supposed to hold it. Although he is younger and fitter than most and fluent in five languages, the Polish army rejects his application. Many others are knocked back, too. Kubush hears they are refusing to enlist Jews, but Mindla doesn't care why, she is just happy he won't be leaving. The thought of a single night away from her husband again is unbearable.

Kubush and the other men at the camp work at the local kolkhoz, in exchange for food. The collective farm pays them ten ounces of millet each day and some potatoes and a little cabbage on Sundays. On a good week they may get an onion as well. It is gruelling work in the icy conditions and even with gloves his hands blister picking up the frozen potatoes through the snow, but it keeps him and his family alive.

Some days the weather is so fierce the men are unable to work. When the buran arrives, there is little choice but to stay shut inside the cattle car. These cyclonic winds whip up ice particles from the tundra and pummel them into anything they meet. A man caught in the whistling buran is sure to die a painful death. There is, however, a silver lining to the harsh climate. Hitler's men are no match for the brutal Russian winter. Deep mud and frozen fields are making his advance impossible, with tanks bogged and many unable to survive the deep freeze.

One night the Polish soldiers light a bonfire and invite the evacuees to join them for home-brewed vodka around the fire to celebrate, but deep down they all know that when the spring arrives the hydra will be back with many heads.

•

The new year ticks over with little fanfare, but on 15 January 1942, Anders announces a plan to move the army's main base towards Tashkent, two thousand kilometres to the south. Civilians are able to travel with them.

Mindla and Kubush have heard much about the exotic city of Tashkent, located a world away beyond vast Kazakhstan to the south, a hop-skip to the Chinese border. Word around the camp is it is a land of bread and endless sunshine. Nobody can predict how long this war will last, but Mindla knows they won't survive another winter in Totskoye. Her eyes turn to the little boy whose skin hasn't seen sun for longer than she can remember.

That very evening, buoyed by hope and the promise of warmth, a long train of coupled cattle cars begins rolling towards Tashkent, perhaps this time towards a lasting freedom. As they pass over endless miles of desolate steppe and rocky plains no human could call home, Mindla allows her mind to wander to the glorious ancient bazaars and colourful eastern markets that await her. She imagines fruit she's never tasted before with juice that will drip down her chin, and spices so rich and real she can almost smell them. She relies on daydreams to carry her through the long weeks it takes to travel to the faraway city.

Turquoise skies greet them, yes, but so too does the tail end of war. An epidemic of typhus has beaten them to Tashkent and the exhausted refugees spend their first day in quarantine, waiting to be disinfected. It takes hours, and when Mindla's turn comes, officials order her to strip off and enter a public bath to be cleansed, while her clothes are washed in giant vats of chemicals. Gad's skin itches for days after the dousing and he cries himself to sleep.

Mindla's daydreams of a splendid, cosmopolitan metropolis are a far cry from the reality of yet another temporary home. The city is broad and flat, a rabbit warren of dirt alleys lined with single-storey homes that easily confuse the new arrivals.

Temporary camps housing the thousands of refugees are dotted around the city, while some are billeted a room in the cramped mud huts of the local Uzbeks. Mindla, Kubush and Gad live in one of the camps, a dust bowl dotted with canvas tents. Each day the routine is the same; Kubush picks cotton or vegetables on nearby farms while Mindla scours the streets for food. With many new arrivals, food is hard to come by and long queues form for bread and dumplings. Water is plentiful but tastes like dust. Thieves and pickpockets ply a roaring trade.

Mindla wonders if she will ever sleep soundly again.

Each transport of refugees brings more disease, and it is not the heady scent of Middle Eastern or Asian spices that lingers in the air, but the stench from vats of disinfectant.

It isn't long before the Anders army is on the road again, and so too is the caravan of refugees in their care.

The Russian government can no longer feed and provide for them; they have failed to deliver much-needed equipment, boots, clothing and munitions to Anders and his men, and have supplied barely enough food to feed the thousands of Polish civilians travelling with them. They are handed over to the care of the British, which means a long journey on foot to British-occupied Persia. Anders and his men will guard the oil fields while the refugees will be processed and repatriated to various parts of the British Empire.

It is not a journey for the faint-hearted or weak, but Persia, they are told, is well organised under the joint command of British and American forces. Food is plentiful and from there, the British will find them a new home somewhere under the King's rule.

Nothing but hope fuels every blistered footstep along dirt roads and mountainous tracks through Afghanistan and into Persia.

'Soon we will see the sea,' Mindla coaxes Gad whenever he is tired and doesn't want to go on. The promise of seeing the ocean for the very first time buoys him.

She marvels at how the young boy is mature beyond his five years, but then, what else does he know? His life has been a miserable rollercoaster of suffering.

Many don't survive the long journey but Kubush, Mindla and Gad are among the lucky ones who arrive in Tehran safely months later. The Persian paradise they've been promised mostly lives up to its name. Even in winter it's nothing but blue sky as far as the eye can see and red desert sand that rolls into green lawns and towering cypress trees. General Anders is a man of his word, and the joint forces look after those who survive the brutal journey. When they arrive, they are taken to civilian camps with food, spacious tents and hot showers. Anywhere they can take a breath and feel the sun on their back is paradise after where they've come from.

Almost immediately on arrival at the camp, they go through a familiar routine: clothes are boiled and disinfected to remove the lice. But when the first food rations are handed out, Mindla knows they have made the right decision. Gad's eyes can barely take in the delights before him: cheese, plump sugary dates oozing sweetness, bread, tea and even fresh meat. Gad sucks on the dates, devouring them as if they are lollies, and Mindla happily shares her ration with him just to see him so happy. Paradise indeed.

Camp life is mostly mundane, until one day Kubush spies an opportunity. There is a little stage from which speeches are delivered and communications shared from the joint forces to the refugees. Kubush can't help but dust off some old tricks and bring a smile to the faces of the camp children whenever he gets the chance. Dozens of youngsters are calling this camp their temporary home. It fills his heart with joy to put on a little show every now and then to entertain them. Silly expressions, magic tricks and wobbly walks tease out the most joyful laughter. Seeing the children lost in magic and briefly happy helps heal the broken adults, too.

They are almost free, but not yet home. It takes several months for the paperwork to be processed, but at long last it's ready and they steel themselves for one last journey. To Africa.

CHAPTER THIRTY-ONE

Africa, 1943

'Will there be elephants, Mama?' Gad asks.

'Oh, moy malysh – *my baby* – will there be elephants? Of course, there'll be elephants in Africa!' she says, curling her hands into a pretend telescope that she cocks to her eye.

'I can see them now, their long trunks swaying from side to side, tigers prowling and giraffes with necks that stretch so high into the sky their noses touch the clouds, and roly-poly hippopotamuses with their big bellies ready to gobble you up!'

Gad giggles as she smooths his hair back off his forehead.

'My darling, there are so many animals in Africa we'll have our very own circus!' She grins, cuddling him closer on their makeshift bunk. Over the long years of his short life, the five-year-old has mastered using his imagination to turn darkness into light. Today's make-believe games are helping take their minds off the seasickness. The cork-bottle freighter has been bobbing around in the swell for six days,

243

rocking and rolling all the way from the Arabian Sea, down the windswept east African coast.

Mindla has never stepped foot on a boat, let alone sailed across the ocean, and she battles waves of nausea for days. With nothing but sky and sea on the horizon, the Indian Ocean feels comfortingly out of Hitler's reach.

It is six days after leaving Karachi, where they stopped for supplies, before the ship's watch rings his bell. His clarion call of 'Land ahoy!' is not for the safety of the captain's navigation but for the passengers, desperate to catch the first glimpse of their new home.

Kubush, Mindla and Gad race upstairs and jostle for position on the deck among hundreds of fellow Poles watching the white sandy beaches of Mombasa inch closer. Soon they can make out the jagged outline of palm trees, and then the water around them slowly becomes crystal clear.

The voyage of 2700 miles is almost over. They have been promised paradise so many times, but Mombasa actually is. It is the most beautiful place Mindla has ever seen.

British soldiers mill around the docks, ready to transport the refugees to their new homes.

A soldier holds out his hand to Gad, and the little boy dutifully shakes it in return.

'Welcome to Kenya, Ma'am!' he says to Mindla.

Mindla can't help herself; she plants a kiss on the young man's cheek, just as the many women before her have done. 'A kiss for the King!' she says, beaming. 'Long live the King!'

'Long live the King,' he replies, and laughs.

For Mindla, Gad and Kubush, home is a thatched roof hut at Camp Nyabyeya in Masindi, over the Kenyan border in neighbouring Uganda. The settlement is nestled between thick forest on one side, and acres of farming fields that roll down to Lake Albert on the other. In contrast to the knee-deep snows of Totskoye and the stinging desert sands of Tashkent and Persia, they really have arrived in the promised land.

Mindla instantly feels at home at Camp Nyabyeya. For all intents and purposes, it is a bustling Polish village in the heart of Africa, where two thousand Poles are piecing together their broken lives. Nobody here has been spared the hand of the Nazis.

The first wave of refugees has built a paradise from paddocks: hundreds of huts, a communal kitchen, a school, a church and a temple, and even a community stage where they now gather to sing and dance and show movies. Most speak Polish and Mindla is instantly comforted by the warmth and familiarity of the language from home.

At first glance, their thick mud-walled hut, made from a crude daub of lime and straw, belies the surprisingly comfortable interior. It has two large rooms and a kitchen area with windows looking out over the fields, and their beds have mosquito nets. It is heaven.

A gift from the American and British forces is waiting for them on the pine-slab kitchen table. There's a bundle of new clothes, a pile of books, and a little radio to keep in touch with news from the front. Such kindness brings Mindla to tears. It is the first time she has allowed herself to cry since they began this wretched journey and the relief of having a place to call home is overwhelming. Kubush wraps his arms around her waist. 'We made it,' he whispers, kissing her forehead. 'We made it.'

Their first order once they have settled in is to attend a briefing by the camp commandant. The rules of Camp Nyabyeya are relatively simple, he explains, and if everyone follows them, they will each live a happy and abundant life.

'Everyone must earn their keep,' the commandant says. 'We all work on the farms and around the village, so we can all eat.'

Then he bends down to speak directly to the children. 'You must listen, children, this is very important,' he says, shushing them quiet. 'You must never disturb the animals.' He waves a finger at them. 'Never, never, never!'

'When you see an elephant, you tiptoe away quietly. Do not approach him, nor the leopards or the hyenas. And, please children, never *ever* go to the lake without an adult, or the crocodiles will use your bones for toothpicks!'

Lake Albert is a popular place for swimming, especially on hot summer days, but along with fish, birds and the odd hippo, Nile crocodiles also call the warm waters home. The commandant tells the children a gruesome story about a little boy who snuck away from camp and went swimming alone and was never seen again. Is it a true story? It doesn't matter. It has the desired effect, scaring the little mites into following the rules.

The camp is made up of eight little settlements or larger villages connected by a main road, officially called Do What You Want Street. The Horowitzes live in the village of Monkey Grove, and Mindla soon learns why. The street backs on to a forest filled with the creatures who greet her at the kitchen window every morning looking for food scraps. If she doesn't keep the window closed, she finds them in her cupboards and under her bed.

Some believe the monkeys are pests, but Mindla secretly adores them, patting their soft fur at every chance.

'Mangoes, juicy mangoes,' a voice sings at the door. In the two days since arriving, Mindla and Kubush are overwhelmed by the generosity of their neighbours, who have brought vegetables, fresh milk and even meat. For dinner on their first night in camp Mindla had a piece of steak so thick she could barely get her mouth around it. If it was her last meal, she'd die happy.

Kubush opens the door expecting to find one of the local Ugandans. He is not at all prepared for who he sees.

'What took you so long to get here, Mr Kubush?' Faivel says, grinning.

'Faivel! You schmuck!' Kubush laughs, embracing the little man, whose tanned skin has benefited from the glorious African sun. 'When did you get here? Come in!'

Over many hours, many cups of coffee, and the odd shot of bootleg whisky, they make up for lost time. They swap stories of wretched hunger and sleepless nights in flea-ridden places they'd rather forget.

Not long after they said their goodbyes in Bialystok, Faivel was rounded up and sent by the Russians to a gulag near the Ural Mountains. He was released during the amnesty and followed a similar path to freedom with another wave of Polish refugees. But thankfully that's now all in the past, and neither man will dwell on previous hardships, fully aware that they are luckier than most just to have survived.

Faivel is living at the nearby Camp Koji and working at the local hospital, cleaning and doing all of the odd jobs needed to keep the place running. He has a soft spot for the nurses and they share a soft spot for him.

'Camp life is good, Kubush. There is plenty of food for everyone and you can make money here. I will take you hunting crocodiles one day!'

He suggests the family make their way to the camp theatre once they are settled.

'The children's choir is really quite something and you definitely won't want to miss the weekly women's auxiliary play.' He pulls a face, grimacing playfully, then a thought seems to occur to him. 'The one thing this place could do with is a good circus,' he says with a twinkle in his eye.

•

The family settle in to a routine quickly. Each day, Gad joins the other camp children for school lessons while Kubush works at a sugar and maize farm. Mother Nature has blessed this African heartland with rich soil and a tropical climate perfect for growing just about anything, and the Poles have planted large swathes of corn, potatoes, carrots and cabbage. The fields farmed by the community are lush, green and highly productive thanks to bore water from Lake Albert, which also supports a herd of cattle, so there is no shortage of milk or meat, either.

Mindla relishes the weather. The consistently humid days offer very little variation and even the rains, when they come, are warm – she loves the predictability. One by one she meets her neighbours, women all of a similar age whose conversations remind her of chatting with Jadzia and Eva. She asks everyone she meets if they have news from Warsaw. Mindla has heard stories about the ghetto and the death camps, but she struggles to believe they can be true.

Once a week she visits the commandant to ask if any new arrivals are coming, but there's never any news. She prays that her Papa and Jadzia and Eva and Yakov will arrive here one day. Oh, how Yakov would love these sprawling farms and the wild jungle around them. But her heart tells her not to hope.

'They're all gone, Mindla, you must forget about them,' says Raizel, who lives a few huts away. Raizel was a seamstress back in Poland and she has been sourcing fabric and cutting patterns for many of the women. She has offered to make Mindla a new dress to replace her polka-dot cotton one and white blouse, which have long seen better days.

Raizel's handiwork couldn't have come at a better time because Mindla's waist is rapidly expanding. The queasy tummy and waves of nausea she battled on the ship do not subside and it soon becomes obvious why. Little Maks arrives safely on 28 July 1943, delivered at the nearby Masindi hospital. With its whitewashed walls and linoleum floor, and a doctor and two nurses on hand, it is luxury in comparison to the delivery of Gad on the kitchen floor at 17 Muranowska Street, half a world away in Warsaw. Like his big brother, Maks has fine blond hair and big blue eyes, and tiny little fingers he wraps tightly around Mindla's pinky. She is instantly smitten, and so too is Kubush, who celebrates with gusto back at the camp.

On the same night Maks is making his way into the world, the Allies bomb the city of Hamburg, all but destroying it. It is a key leap forward in the war and Mindla thinks it is a good omen. After so much death and sadness, maybe, just maybe, life is taking a turn for the better.

Gad easily befriends the other camp children and together the rascals make up for lost time. From dawn until dusk they follow their imaginations wherever they may lead, using the rusty camp bikes to explore beyond the forest boundary, getting up to all sorts of mischief, reclaiming what's left of the childhood Hitler stole from them.

The rubbery vines of the towering liana trees make wonderful jungle swings and more than one cubby house is pieced together from leftover nails and scraps of wood. No-one begrudges the children these adventures, as long as they are home in time for dinner.

But when it's harvest time at the camp farm, it's all-hands-on-deck and the children must help out too. Gad goes to 'work' with Kubush, riding the tractor and helping load and unload the trucks. Day by day the dark shadow of war and suffering fades from their little minds.

Faivel is right about the entertainment at the camp. A brave attempt at a children's choir and some widows reciting Charles Dickens does not a show make! The dour faces in the audience say as much.

Faivel and Kubush get busy rehearsing, finding it doesn't take long to shake off the circus cobwebs. To perform, they must get approval from the commandant, who immediately gives his blessing and insists they begin as soon as possible, leading them to believe that he can't stomach another croaking rendition of 'The White Cliffs' either.

The night before they are to take to the stage, the pair knock on doors and spread the word through the villages. 'The circus is coming to town!' Not surprisingly, the little theatre is jam-packed when it comes to showtime. Children sit on one another's laps on the ground in front of the stage, and their parents fill row after row behind them until there is standing room only at the back. Mindla is gently rocking baby Maks, who is soothed by sucking her pinky.

Just before sunset, it is showtime.

In his biggest voice, the camp commandant introduces them. 'Ladies and gentlemen, please welcome the Circus Nyabyeya!' He won't be joining Ringling Brothers any time soon, but it does the job nonetheless.

Kubush and Faivel run out on stage and take a bow, then it's down to the serious work of making everyone laugh. Kubush has taught Faivel the routines he learnt with Karandash in Russia, and their impersonations of Hitler win over the crowd immediately. Then they call upon the old routines of the Circus Staniewski, knowing they are guaranteed crowd pleasers.

The two men fall into routine so smoothly it's as if they've never been apart – Kubush knowing when to swing a plank of wood so it just misses Faivel's head, or the precise moment to turn their legs to jelly simultaneously, melting to the floor as they walk. They have no costumes and no make-up other than a dot of Mindla's favourite red lipstick on their noses, but it doesn't matter, the language of slapstick is universal. For both men, the real magic is happening offstage as the infectious laughter of the children spreads happiness through the theatre.

At the end of their routine, the audience gives the two men a standing ovation. Thunderous applause warms everyone's hearts. Kubush glances down to see Gad clapping with such excitement his little hands might fly right off, and it almost brings him to tears. No audience has ever meant more to him than this one. His son. Kubush turns to Faivel and catches his eye, and as they take one more bow, Faivel pushes the back of Kubush's legs, sending him tumbling. It is well-rehearsed spontaneity of course, but the children squeal with delight. Faivel revels in the spotlight, taking bow after bow before the adoring audience, then runs for dear life when Kubush pretends to angrily chase him offstage. Backstage, the smile on Faivel's face is wider than anything he could paint with make-up.

For the next week, the camp's children flock to Faivel everywhere he goes, and their mothers, who've never bothered to give him the time of day, suddenly stop to congratulate him on his performance. For the rest of his time in Masindi, Faivel walks ten feet tall.

CHAPTER THIRTY-TWO

1 May 1945

It is late on a Tuesday evening and the monsoon season has begun.

Kubush is sound asleep, exhausted from working around the clock over the past week to get the last of the maize sown. In the two years they've been in Africa, he and Mindla have come to know the seasons like clockwork, and when mustiness hangs in the air, the rains are just days away. They finished sowing yesterday just in the nick of time, because this afternoon the kusi rains arrived.

The cooler night still offers no relief from the sticky humidity of the day, however. Mindla tries to sleep but she is distracted by a squadron of mosquitoes dive-bombing her protective net. She is annoyed to be robbed of precious rest. Maks is a toddler now and unlike his older brother, Gad, he barely sits still during the day. The robust little boy is quick on his feet and constantly demands her attention. She has her hands full with a new baby too: little Henry, now six months old.

She lies still, focusing on the rain, hoping the rhythmic downpour will take her mind off the bugs, but just as she settles, a new noise disturbs the silence, whooping and yelling. Someone is having a party. Mindla is furious, and desperately hopes the noise won't wake Henry, sleeping in the crib beside her.

A car horn adds to the hijinks, now waking Kubush too. 'What on earth is going on?' he says, pulling his trousers on over his underwear. 'Bloody fools.'

The commotion continues and Kubush hurries to the door intent on giving the lads a piece of his mind, but just as he steps outside a car races up through the darkness, flashing its headlights into the sleepy huts.

'Hitler is dead!' the men yell, 'Hitler is dead!' Within a few minutes the entire village is awake. A few hours earlier, German President Karl Dönitz announced the death of Hitler on Hamburg radio and news has spread quickly around the world.

Mindla doesn't know whether to laugh or cry, and in the downpour, she does both. In the darkness, a lone voice begins a spontaneous rendition of *Dabrowski's Mazurka*, the Polish national anthem. One by one the villagers emerge onto the street and join in the choir of joy and grief. Kubush slaps his neighbours on the back and they embrace one another with delight. The men's deep voices carry the motherland's song.

Mindla and the women from the surrounding huts link arms and sing too.

For the rest of the night, Do What You Want Street lives up to its name, alive with music and dancing and farmwork-weary men swigging home-brewed vodka. Not even the rains will dampen their spirits. Thank goodness the maize has been sown, because no-one will be fit to work in the morning.

It's not so much that the exiled Poles are dancing on Hitler's grave, although they are perfectly justified in doing so; they are singing for the souls they will never see again. Giving voice to the sisters and brothers, mothers and fathers, daughters and sons the Nazis stole from them.

Mindla sneaks away from the celebrations, seeking the quiet of the hut. The news casts her mind back to her own family and it is a bittersweet feeling not knowing whether her beloved Papa, or her brothers and sisters, are dead or alive.

Miraculously, all three of her beautiful boys have slept soundly through the ruckus. She studies their faces as she peels off her soaking clothes, marvelling at how angelic they look when asleep. She reaches over and gives each of her precious sons another kiss goodnight. Gad and Maks top and tail a single bed. 'Sweet dreams,' she whispers in their ears. For the first time in years, she knows these are not just hollow words. From this day forward, her children will never have to face Hitler's evil hand. She rests her head on the pillow and falls into a deep sleep, knowing that this wretched war will soon be over.

PART III

After the War

CHAPTER THIRTY-THREE

Italy, 1948

'Shoosh, Henry!' Gad whispers, planting a clammy hand across his youngest brother's mouth.

The three Horowitz boys and a handful of camp kids crouch behind a flimsy wall that forms one side of an elaborate film set, their ears cupped to the partition as they listen intently. None of the children are game to speak let alone move a muscle, except little Henry, who has no idea what all of the fuss is about.

On the other side of the wafer-thin plywood is a majestic fifteenth-century cathedral, resplendent with fake frescoes and replica marble fittings that cleverly imitate the real thing. Dozens of cast and film-crew are now in position ready to roll, waiting for the director to arrive. 'Silence on the set!' the assistant shouts, 'he's here.' Gad clamps his hand a little bit tighter over Henry's mouth and shoots Maks a piercing dagger that says now is not the time for hijinks. Barely a breath can be heard as the assistant claps the slate together to begin filming.

'Action!' he yells.

'The dead must not place too great a burden on the living,' the actor bellows. 'It is my belief that everything, even death, can be turned into profit.'

The boys can't see him but his voice is unmistakable, the rich, leathery resonance bouncing off the walls of the hollow sound stage as he delivers his monologue. Gad closes his eyes and takes in every word of the deep, whisky-smooth enunciation. The words almost vibrate through him.

Little more than five millimetres of dusty board separates the children from Orson Welles, one of the biggest movie stars in the world. He is filming *Prince of Foxes* at the Cinecittà studios in Italy, Europe's biggest film studio. Built by Mussolini before the war in an attempt to rival Hollywood, the sprawling lot on the outskirts of Rome is now the set of Twentieth Century Fox's highly anticipated film starring Orson Welles and Tyrone Power. It is also the home of three thousand bone-tired war refugees, finally in transit to their permanent homes. In the hangar beside *Prince of Foxes*, preparations are beginning for the filming of Metro-Goldwyn-Mayer's epic historical drama *Quo Vadis*.

The children don't move a muscle as Welles perfectly delivers every line of his character, the Machiavellian Prince Cesare Borgia. Within minutes he is done. 'Cut!' the assistant yells, banging down the clapper again.

The boys catch a fleeting glimpse of the Hollywood icon as he breezes past them on his way back to his dressing room. He is close enough that they can almost reach out and touch him, but no fool would dare, except maybe Henry, whose hands are being held so tight he can't.'

The children hang around the set long after Orson Welles has gone, hoping to catch a glimpse of the movie's other big name, the Hollywood starlet Wanda Hendrix. Today they are out of luck. The raven-haired beauty has already left, but she'll be back again tomorrow, as will the starstruck children who spend every waking minute of their day lost in the magical world of movies.

Mindla and Kubush are happy to let the boys roam the vast lot because it is impossible to keep them cooped up in the storage room turned dormitory that is currently their home.

For six months now they've been stuck in Cinecittà, a no-man's-land of the desperate and stateless. Since the end of the war the refugee camps in Africa have been closed and although the family has been granted visas to start a new life in Australia, the wait feels interminable.

Faivel was also granted a visa and has already sailed, along with a handful of other fortunate families. They have all been sponsored by a butcher in Melbourne, Julius Redlich, whose brother Ernst was living in the camps in Africa.

Faivel sends letters to them regularly. 'I wait for you impatiently,' he writes. 'I am very happy here, and you will be too [. . .] in Australia you can settle well, you can have your own business and not work very hard.'

Each letter, although happily received, makes Mindla and Kubush all the more impatient to leave.

After years of running, they long to settle in one place and desperately hope this journey will be the last they ever make. When they arrived in Genoa they expected to stay one or two days at the most before boarding their ship to Melbourne, but instead they found themselves eight miles outside Rome holed up in this makeshift refugee camp with three thousand others headed for new lives in Australia, Canada and England. And no sign of departure.

Their accommodation is an old film storage room that has been turned into living quarters they share with 140 others. Their beds are coarse jute sacks stuffed with straw that itches their skin. They are packed together so tightly that their noses are barely centimetres apart, and they all share one bathroom.

Frustrated, Kubush sends letter after letter to the director of the International Refugee Organization. 'We have nothing but a thin blanket to keep us warm in this freezing winter,' he writes. 'The conditions here are simply horrific. In some respects, they are worse than the Russian camps even during the war. For instance, the hygienic state of the lavatory is such that it can only be called a shame to every civilised standard. It is used day and night by 140 people with no light. Though we have electricity we have no light bulbs, and it is awfully dirty.'

Kubush is also becoming increasingly desperate because the precious pennies he saved in Africa in the hope of starting a new life in Melbourne are running out fast now that he has to buy food and new winter clothes for his family. Many people around them are becoming ill.

'We do not belong in this place, we are prisoners,' he complains. 'I am sure that none of those who cause us to live under the abovementioned conditions would even dream of spending one night that way. I'm fighting for my fundamental human rights. I am supposed to be a free man. I can only appeal to your honour as being the protector of the poor and homeless and supplicate you to do all that is possible so as to ensure our further transfer to Australia at the earliest occasion.'

Each week they steel themselves and line up outside the director's office, waiting for the transport lists to be posted up on the wall. And each week they return, deflated, to the storage room where Mindla buries her head in the jute bed and sobs. She is desperate to step off this endless emotional rollercoaster of hope followed by crushing disappointment.

Finally, on 1 February 1949, a breakthrough.

Kubush lines up, patiently waiting his turn to check the list. Mindla doesn't bother coming; she's almost given up hope. When he reaches the front of the line he runs his fingers slowly down the carefully typed manifest.

'Horky, Horodynski, Horoszko,' he says, reading the names aloud to himself. 'Horowitz! Horowitz! That's me.' He clutches his hat and races into the director's office to sign the paperwork. He is handed an envelope of documents and the precious tickets they will need to sail at the end of the week.

Kubush stuffs the papers safely into the pocket of his coat and runs back to the dormitory, spitting out the good news to Mindla, who is busying herself by helping the other women make beds and clean the filthy hall.

'We are sailing!' he says beaming. 'At last we are sailing!'

On 3 February they board the *Toscana*, a white beacon of hope that sails the Horowitz family and 826 others across the seas to a new home at the bottom of the world.

As the morning sun rises over Port Phillip Bay, Mindla and Kubush catch their first glimpse of Melbourne. Streetlights twinkle in the pink dawn and a grey shadow, which they assume is the city's buildings, hangs gently on the horizon. A light southerly breeze off the water freshens tired faces as the weary couple share a cigarette on the otherwise empty deck. The boys are still sound asleep down below and their parents have no intention of waking them, savouring the brief serenity.

Kubush wraps his arms around Mindla's waist and draws her in close. He can smell the salt in her hair. It has been an epic voyage getting here from Italy, navigating through the Suez Canal, to Egypt, Ceylon and across the rolling swell of the Indian Ocean to Fremantle, then finally around the Great Australian Bight to Melbourne. It makes Mindla queasy just thinking about it. Neither will ever set foot on a boat again.

'No looking back,' Kubush whispers to his wife, who is

unusually quiet. 'No good comes from mourning what we cannot change.' She nods her head in agreement.

It is 14 March 1949, Labour Day in Victoria, and the *Toscana* is steaming up the bay after coming through the heads before daybreak. By mid-morning, the repurposed hospital ship docks at Station Pier. While Kubush organises their luggage, Mindla herds the boys together and does a last-minute check for anything they may have left behind.

They disembark wearing the finest Italian clothes their dwindling pennies could buy.

'You only get one chance to make a first impression,' Kubush tells his boys. He stops to buy a newspaper from the kiosk at the end of the long pier as they amble towards the taxi rank. Kubush is fluent in Polish, Russian and Lithuanian, he knows a little German and has learnt enough Swahili to get by in the camps in Africa, but he struggles to grasp the attendant's strange Australian accent. It's not British and it's not American, it curls awkwardly somewhere in between. Clearly there is much to learn here.

With the paper tucked under his arm, and a handful of change, he turns to walk away, but Gad is beside him wide-eyed and almost dribbling at a large poster advertising ice cream.

'Papa, can I have a Peters?' he asks, reading the sign.

Given the cool morning has turned into an unseasonably warm autumn day, and Kubush is in a celebratory mood, he returns to the kiosk and points to the poster, holding up three fingers to indicate what he wants. The man nods his head in understanding and smiles.

Gad works his tongue around and around the vanilla ice cream in methodical circles, licking up every last drop. 'It's the most delicious thing I've ever tasted,' he says.

Henry and Maks nod in agreement, licking their melting ice creams as fast as they can. As they lose control the liquid slides down their cones and onto their fingers in a glorious, sticky mess. They all laugh and Mindla digs in her purse to find a tissue to mop up. Kubush glances at the front page of the *Sun* while they wait for their cab. 'The King of England has had an operation on his leg,' he tells Mindla. 'He is recovering in hospital.' Mindla nods in appreciation of any news from Europe.

'The war has taken a toll on us all,' she replies.

Kubush scans the paper, observing that there is a horse race at Flemington Racecourse that seems to be of more interest to the Australian population than the king's health. A three-year-old filly named Lady Pirouette is the favourite for the sprint. Kubush flicks ahead, looking for jobs, making a mental note of an ad for double-breasted jackets at Roger David menswear, and one for Pelaco shirts.

The taxi arrives as the children are finishing their cones. By the time Kubush has loaded their luggage into the boot of the car, Mindla has cleaned up her sons' fingers and faces and they are ready for the drive to their new home. They head down Beaconsfield Parade and onto the Esplanade through St Kilda.

'Look!' Henry squeals as they approach the gaping mouth of Luna Park. The boys press their faces against the car window, their eyes following the curves of the rickety wooden roller-coaster up and down and around in circles.

'It's a giant clown, Papa!' Gad cries. 'Please, Papa, can we go there?' he begs.

'Not today, but one day soon,' he promises.

It's only a few more minutes before they arrive at 29 Worthing Road in Highett, a pretty red clinker-brick house with a neat front garden and extensive back yard. The yard is a little overgrown and in need of some attention but Mindla is quickly planning a vegetable garden and maybe a chicken coop to make good use of the space.

'Welcome to your new home, boys,' Kubush says as the three of them kick off their shoes and socks and frolic in the calf-length grass.

Mindla sits down on the back porch and lights a cigarette while watching them play. She peels off her coat and cardigan, allowing the sun to warm her skin. A smile creeps across her face seeing the boys tearing off handfuls of green grass and tossing them at one another in a playfight.

Somewhere between the Suez Canal and the Red Sea she turned thirty, but she feels so much older. She has spent her entire adult life running, never able to plant roots, never able to truly settle. Always looking over her shoulder. But now she is home. Australia has welcomed them with open arms and invited them to begin a new life. No more running, no more hiding. She thinks of Warsaw, and her beloved Mama. Chana Levin could never have imagined a house as beautiful as this.

Mindla remembers the lines on her mother's face and her fine hands covered in flour, the smell of her bread cooking in the oven. A stabbing pain pierces her heart as she thinks of her family. But she must bury those images somewhere deep inside her heart. She must lock their beautiful faces away in a box in the back of her mind and never let them out, otherwise the sadness will destroy her. Darkness and despair will consume her soul. Hatred will poison her blood. Like Kubush says, no good comes from looking back. Never look back.

A squeal brings her back to this yard in the middle of Melbourne, a city of pretty gardens and green grass, of wide streets and funny-looking trams and pretty beaches and ice creams. It is laughter she is hearing, joyful laughter. Maks has tossed a snail in his little brother's face.

She stubs the cigarette out and heads inside to make the beds and unpack their meagre belongings.

CHAPTER THIRTY-FOUR

November 1949

Mindla is oblivious to the kettle whistling on the stove. Steam inches up the wallpaper towards the ceiling but she is so distracted by the little girl standing in front of her she doesn't notice.

Jadzia, the sister she has missed and longed for all these years, has arrived in Australia with a husband and daughter. It is hard to believe she is here in her kitchen; harder still to comprehend that the child and husband she has brought with her are not her family from Warsaw. They are complete strangers to Mindla.

'The kettle!' Jadzia exclaims and the two of them giggle at Mindla's absent-mindedness. Mindla passes a cup of coffee across the laminate tabletop and takes her sister's hand. Mindla can't stop staring at her beautiful sister, it is as if she's seen a ghost. She reaches out and they hug again; they've hardly stopped hugging since Jadzia's ship docked earlier that morning.

'Hanna, darling, why don't you run outside and play with Henry,' Jadzia says softly, but the shy child has no intention of leaving her mother's side. They've just arrived after the long journey across the seas at a strange house with unfamiliar faces.

Mindla knows she will come around in time. And they have all the time in the world.

'It's lovely having a little girl in the house,' Mindla says, gazing at Hanna's chocolate pigtails and wide blue eyes. She has to stop herself from pinching the child's rosy cheeks. 'She looks like Mama.'

Morning sun streams through the kitchen window, illuminating every line on the sisters' faces. It's been nine years since they've seen one another. Nine years and a lifetime. Tragedy has aged them both prematurely but Mindla sees a familiar spark in Jadzia's almond eyes. Mindla could barely believe it when she received a letter from the International Refugee Organization telling her that Jadzia was alive and hoping to settle in Australia. The IRO asked if Mindla would sponsor her. What a question. Of course! She dropped everything and ran straight to the local post office, wiring an answer back immediately. She has counted down the days ever since and now Jadzia is finally here.

Their coffee gets cold as Mindla scoops a pile of flour out of a large tin and deposits it onto the kitchen table, separating it into two mounds. Jadzia cracks an egg into hers and begins working the flour and egg together. They will cook and talk, and share their secrets across the kitchen table, just like they used to do in Warsaw.

'As soon as I heard the whistle I knew,' Jadzia begins, choosing her words carefully in Hanna's presence. Mindla knows her poor sister has replayed this scene a thousand times over in her mind. 'I shouldn't have gone out so early,' she says, shaking her head. 'I'll never forgive myself.'

'Henry, why don't you take Hanna outside to see the chickens and find me some eggs,' Mindla says, gently ushering the children out the back door. When they hear the little ones giggling, Jadzia's shoulders relax and she begins to peel away the layers of grief.

'I woke to find the cupboards almost bare and it was my turn to use my ration card,' Jadzia explains. 'I ducked out to see if I could find a shop for some ersatz coffee and bread while Siva was asleep. I was so hungry I wasn't thinking straight. I didn't notice the street was empty. I turned the corner into Nalewki Street, hoping I'd be early in the queue, and it was only then I looked up.'

Jadzia shudders as she continues to talk, kneading the layers of her life into the pierogi dough.

'I saw a woman in the back of a cattle truck. I knew immediately I was in danger. I turned on my heels, praying they hadn't seen me, and ran, but it was too late.

'The soldier screamed at me. He grabbed my arm and poked the barrel of his gun into my ribs. I begged him and pleaded with him that there'd been a mistake. "I do not live here. I live on Muranowska. I have papers. I am here for food, for my baby." But he had no interest in my story. He was hunting Jews and I was the perfect prey.

'He tossed me in the back of the truck like a rag doll and the next I knew I was at Skarzysko-Kamienna. We worked day and night in the Nazis' factory making their filthy bombs and bullets.'

Tears well in Jadzia's eyes. 'They shot a man standing right beside me,' she tells Mindla. 'The SS roamed the factory constantly and randomly shot workers who hadn't filled their daily quotas. It was impossible to make enough bullets to satisfy them. I could feel his blood in my hair. I didn't even know his name.' Stifling a sob, she continues. 'Most days my fingers bled, but I knew I had to keep going. We were so hungry. If we were lucky they gave us a scrap of mouldy bread each morning and a half cup of dirty black coffee. More dirt than coffee. The Nazis promised that work would set us free, and I prayed that the harder I worked the sooner I would return home to Avraham and Siva. Of course, they lied, the bastards. When Skarzysko-Kamienna was liquidated, I was transported to an equally horrific place, the Hasag munitions camp near Czestochowa. I guess I am lucky, though, as those who didn't make the list for Czestochowa were executed or transported to Auschwitz.

'Some poor souls were kept behind to dig up the rotting bodies of the Jews already murdered, and incinerate them.' She shakes her head at the thought of such horror. 'They were murdered too so none of the Nazi secrets would be told. I was then moved to Bergen-Belsen, and then to Türkheim, a sub-camp of Dachau.

'At Dachau they shaved my head. I was no longer Mrs Jadzia Ksiazenicer nee Levin, wife of Avraham and mother of Siva, but instead prisoner #143838. Just a nameless bag of skin and bones. There was nothing left for them to take.'

The thought of Avraham and Siva is too much and she breaks down. 'They're gone, all of them gone,' she wails.

Tears run down Mindla's face too as she embraces her sister. 'It's not your fault, Jadzia. It's not your fault. Thank God you met Samuel.'

Jadzia wipes her face with a hanky and squeezes Mindla's arm gratefully. She returns to the soft dough and pummels it with the back of her hand, pushing it back and forth. It is a welcome distraction. 'We were both clearing trees in the same labour gang,' she says, swallowing the grief down hard and changing tack. 'He caught my eye because he was more robust than the other men who were mere skeletons with see-through skin stretched over them. I wondered how he managed to stay so strong when he worked harder than any other man I had seen there.

'I often saw him breaking up his pathetic ration of bread and sharing it with the men who weren't faring so well, knowing that if the Germans caught him, they'd take his ration away and delight in watching him starve. When the guards weren't watching we shared snippets of our story. Samuel told me he had been a very successful businessman before the war. He ran a confectionary factory in Lodz. He survived the Lodz ghetto, Auschwitz and Sachsenhausen, before arriving in Dachau. Over the months we slaved alongside one another, he revealed that he had suffered great heartbreak too, losing his wife, Esther, and two daughters, Monika and Lea, to the gas chambers at Chelmno.

'Initially I think we were bonded by loss, but somehow a love grew. I felt safe around Samuel. I was drawn to his optimism, he seemed so certain of the future and when he smiled others smiled around him too.

'We always talked about what we would do when we got out, not if. They were silly dreams but it helped us get through the long days. Deep down I didn't believe we'd ever leave alive. Dachau smelt of death and disease but we'd almost become immune to it. When the Americans arrived, they told us they could smell the decaying bodies long before they marched through the camp gates. Imagine, Mindla, that you've become so used to death you can no longer smell it.

'When we were liberated we vowed that the place would not destroy us, vowed to build a new life together for ourselves and for the ones we loved and lost. We celebrated liberation by marrying, and in doing so denied the Nazis the chance to steal our future too.'

A fleeting smile crosses Jadzia's face. 'Hanna brought love and a happiness to our hearts again. And then we found you, Mindla, the only one left. It is a miracle.'

Mindla nods. 'It is, indeed, a miracle, my sister!' She hugs her again, flour coating them both in the process, and Jadzia whispers, 'Let us never speak of our past again.'

•

'What have we here? A feast! We'll be eating pierogi for the next year,' Kubush says with a grin as he arrives home from the factory to find piles and piles of plump little dumplings covering the kitchen table.

'You two could start a restaurant.'

A strange aroma of braised cabbage and Craven A cigarettes wafts through the house. Mindla glances at the clock; it is already 5:30. They've been so immersed in catching up, they've lost track of time.

Samuel arrives back too, having spent most of the afternoon looking at flats. He thinks he may have found something suitable in Inkerman Street, St Kilda, a little two-bedroom place with a bathroom and a small kitchen. It's not far from Port Phillip Bay, and close to the giant clown park Hanna saw on their drive to the Horowitzes. It is generous of Kubush and Mindla to look after them in the meantime, and Samuel is grateful of the hospitality, but they need to find their own home as soon as possible. It will help them all settle.

Mindla and Jadzia strip off their floury aprons and dust themselves down. Butter is bubbling in a pan, ready to brown the pierogi. Next to it a pot of chicken soup is coming to a gentle simmer.

Mindla hates losing her chickens but the reunion with Jadzia calls for a special dinner. Little Henry was horrified at the sight of his father chopping off the beloved chicken's head yesterday – the entire neighbourhood heard his blood-curdling scream when the thing stumbled towards him minus its head.

'Whisky, anyone?' Kubush asks, pouring them all a drink regardless of the answer. 'To life,' he says, making a toast to absent friends. 'To life,' they chorus.

Over dinner Kubush pulls out every trick in the book to win little Hanna's affection. He starts with funny faces and makes his cutlery disappear, then he finds a coin behind her ear, but none of it impresses her.

He needs to dig deep. Kubush pushes his chair back from the table and pretends he is walking to the sink, then in a split second his legs turn to jelly, wobbling and wiggling, jerking and jiggling like snappy rubber bands. He melts towards the floor, then springs back up again, stiff as a board.

Suddenly, the shy little girl bursts out laughing and her infectious giggle sweeps through the entire table. The boys have seen this trick a hundred times but Hanna's reaction delights them all and it's impossible not to laugh along with her. The more she laughs, the more they laugh too.

'Again!' she orders Kubush, over and over. Kubush smiles to himself, quite proud of his efforts, not just because there is no sound more beautiful than the laughter of a child, but because after all these years he can still make 'em laugh.

Over the years, Kubush and Mindla work hard each day, leaving home at dawn to jobs in various factories, sewing shoulder pads for men's suits, finishing metal buttons or dyeing wool at the nearby mill. Kubush drives taxis, too. In time, they save enough to buy their own business, becoming the proud owners of a milk bar on the corner of Highett and Bluff roads in the bayside suburb of Hampton. Mindla is a natural behind the counter, and Gad is enlisted to help out too.

They all agree Kubush and his limited English are best utilised behind the scenes after he gives a customer asking for cornflakes a tin of Bex tablets instead.

Working hard and continuing to save every penny means they can add shops in St Kilda East, Armadale and Ringwood to the family business. The milk bars are all very successful but there's something stirring in Kubush's soul, some unfinished business.

On weekends at Shul, or at dinner parties, bar mitzvahs or children's birthday celebrations, old habits die hard. Faivel and Kubush can't help putting on a little show. Whether it's magic tricks or silly faces, clowning around and making people laugh is an itch that has to be scratched. So, when Kubush sees an advertisement in the newspaper for auditions for a new television show, curiosity gets the better of him.

CHAPTER THIRTY-FIVE

1959

Mindla is propped against a wooden stool in the bathroom. As she flicks the ash of her cigarette into the sink, she notices a chip in the red varnish on one of her fingernails.

'Klutz,' she scolds herself, reaching around Kubush and into the cabinet to find the little bottle of pillar-box red varnish. It will need to be fixed before they leave.

'What do you think?' Kubush asks.

She leans back onto the stool again in an effort to fully take in his face.

'Turn your head, show me the other side,' she says.

He swivels his face towards her and she studies every inch, carefully checking for any uneven patches. She still loves watching him paint his face, loves the way he gets lost in the art of transformation and the way his brows furrow ever so slightly as he concentrates on perfecting every line.

'You look like a clown,' she says, and grins.

Kubush is leaving nothing to chance. He caught the train to the Myer department store in the city and bought the most expensive face paint money could buy: Mehron, an American brand that all the famous entertainers use. If Mindla knew how much it cost, she'd kill him.

The white pancake sponges on easily enough, although his chiselled jaw has softened over the years and he has jowls he needs to cover, too. At forty-nine, his skin is not as smooth as it used to be and the make-up catches in little creases around his eyes, but he dabs into the feathery cracks with the tip of a finger, smoothing the sticky emulsion. His deep-blue eyes still sparkle the way they did on the night he rescued Mindla and her twisted ankle from the cobblestone street.

He's done this so often he could paint his face in his sleep, but it's been a long time since he's concentrated this hard, making absolutely certain there is not a dot out of place. He dusts some talcum powder gently over the make-up to set it, then puffs a little onto the top of his head to help slide the skull cap on.

'Soon you won't need the cap,' Mindla teases. He is thinning noticeably on top but wispy blond curls still cling to the sides of his head, which he tucks under the skin-toned rubber sheath.

Mindla dots the nail polish onto her fingernail and care-fully covers up the chip. She takes one last glance in the mirror on her way out the door. Her hair is swept back off her forehead and lacquered neatly into place. Her lips are painted red to match her nail polish and she is wearing the navy dress she bought for Henry's bar mitzvah. It's been hanging in the cupboard for a few years but the boat neckline and pleated skirt never go out of fashion.

She tucks an extra cigarette into her purse and clips on a pair of gold earrings as she makes her way out the door. Kubush is wearing a smart brown suit with his shirt unbuttoned loosely at the top so the collar doesn't rub his make-up. His costume, too cumbersome for him to wear while he's driving, is on the back seat of the car. There'll be plenty of time to finish getting dressed before the audition.

When they arrive at the studios of GTV-9 in Bendigo Street, Richmond, a dozen or so performers are already putting the finishing touches to their costumes and routines in a loading bay outside studio nine. A man playing a piano accordion accompanies a troupe of child singers. An older fellow dressed in a hillbilly costume and straw hat carries a guitar. A young clown fiddles with a trolley covered in what looks like equipment for a science experiment. Jugglers and dancers fine-tune their acts. Kubush is noticeably older than them all.

These few are the lucky ones. Hundreds of people applied to audition for *The Tarax Show*, but very few are given the chance.

A man with a clipboard appears at the door of the studio. 'Mr Michael Horowitz,' he calls, 'Michael Horowitz.' Kubush often goes as Michael; he finds it easier because many Australians can't understand his thick, hybrid Polish-Australian accent, and their tongues twist in knots trying to say Kubush.

Everyone can say Michael.

He gathers his costume at the waist and hoists himself up. His red and white checked overcoat stretches over the wide hoop he has around his waist to make him appear round and jolly. He has large fake rubber hands and a tiny red felt hat perched on his head. And he is of course wearing giant shoes. Everything is exaggerated.

'Good luck!' Mindla says. She won't kiss him in case she upsets his make-up.

Kubush is ushered inside the studio, where two men are sitting alone on fold-up wooden chairs in the middle of the set. They have notebooks in their laps. Kubush immediately recognises Ron Blaskett, the ventriloquist who performs in *The Tarax Show* with his dummy Gerry Gee, and the other man introduces himself as the show's producer, Ernie Carroll.

The studio reminds Kubush of Cinecittà. Enormous, darkened spotlights sit cold, waiting for the studio to come to life, and a couple of cameras are in position for the show's next episode. To the back is a small bleacher where dozens of excitable children who have secured a prized ticket to watch the show squash up tight to form the live audience. The wait list is more than a year.

At precisely 5:15 each afternoon, Melbourne children stop to watch *The Tarax Show* on GTV-9. The show's opening jingle is a call to arms through the streets and suburbs to drop whatever you are doing and gather around the television quick smart! Hands washed and faces clean!

> '*Uncle Norman's on his way, we're going to have some fun today,*
> *so put away your worries, you'll soon be feeling fine,*
> *watching* The Tarax Show *each night on Channel Nine.*'

The show's stars are household names, mobbed on the streets: Uncle Norman; King Corky, King of the Kids; Ron Blaskett and Gerry Gee; Joffa Boy; and a young starlet named Patti McGrath. Mindla has purchased dozens of bottles of 'refreshing Tarax' soft drink thanks to the pretty blonde's live advertisements each day. Some of *The Tarax Show* performers also appear on the hugely popular *In Melbourne Tonight* with megastars Graham Kennedy and Bert Newton, which is broadcast later each night from the same studio.

Kubush doesn't waste a second of this opportunity, getting right down to business. He reaches out to shake Ernie Carroll's hand and as soon as the powerful producer's fingers are in his grasp, a flap of red hair flies right off Kubush's head. It's an oldie but a goodie and Ernie and Ron both laugh.

He knows their eyes are studying his every move and it sends a tingle of excitement down his spine. He feels alive when he is making people laugh; most at home hidden under make-up and a heavy costume.

Kubush has only performed for a few minutes when Ernie Carroll stops him.

'Thank you, Michael, that will be enough,' he says. Kubush's heart sinks; he's only performed two or three tricks, barely scraping the surface of the dozens of acts he has up his sleeve.

The two men look at one another and without so much as a whisper between them to share their opinions, Ernie Carroll delivers the news. 'Congratulations, Michael, you're hired.'

Kubush's blood rushes from his feet to his head and it takes all his will to remain standing. He feels he could faint but still manages to take in every word they say.

Ernie Carroll explains that the moment they saw Kubush's make-up and costume, they knew he was a professional. His act is old school – sight gags, mime and physical humour – but he clearly knows how to entertain, and these tricks still make people laugh today. Who doesn't love Abbott and Costello?

Ron Blaskett says he's never seen a presentation like it.

Kubush shakes their hands enthusiastically. 'Thank you,' he says, 'thank you so much. You will not be disappointed.' As he leaves the studio, he turns those spindly legs to jelly one more time, wibble-wobbling all the way out the door. Always the entertainer.

Mindla is nervously smoking a cigarette when she sees him walking towards her.

'Well?' she says. 'That was quick.'

Kubush doesn't say a word, he just nods his head and takes her hand as they walk towards the car park.

'You were too old?' she guesses. 'Was it the costume? We should've got you a new one . . .'

With every step they take she surmises a new reason why Kubush missed out, and he stays tight-lipped until they are well away from the ears of the other performers, whereupon he turns to her with a grin wider than Luna Park.

'I'm going to be on television!' he says, planting a sticky pancake kiss on her lips. It is the happiest day of his life.

That evening they have a special celebration. Mindla prepares a feast of brisket and potato latkes to celebrate the good news, with Faivel their guest of honour. They wash it down with a glass or two of sweet Seppeltsfield Solero, making a toast to Australia – the best country in the world.

The celebrations continue and with each glass comes a new toast: to television, the greatest invention of all time other than Coca-Cola; and to the circus, oh yes, the circus; and to Lala and Bronislaw and to Karandash, the best circus teacher of them all; 'and to the great Faivel Ditkowski!' Faivel quips.

'To you, my friend,' Kubush says, clinking glasses across the table.

But the last toast is saved for the ghosts of the past whose shadows will always gently linger.

'To family,' Mindla says.

'Mazel tov!' they chorus.

EPILOGUE

Pop appeared on *The Tarax Show* on GTV-9 until the mid-1960s, performing under the name Sloppo the Clown. At times he was paired up with another young entertainer named Norman Brown and they were known as Sloppo and Boppo. They did hundreds of performances together. At the time of writing, Norman is fit and well and delighted to share stories about the old days and his and Kubush's adventures on and off television.

Kubush died on 6 September 1989, aged 79. Mindla lived to the grand age of 96, passing away on 25 July 2015.

They are survived by three sons, six grandchildren, nine great-grandchildren and three great-great-grandchildren, none of whom are anywhere near as funny as their seniors.

Gad – or Denis, as he was known – married Mena and had two boys, David and Paul. For many years they lived alongside Mindla and Kubush at their home in Sebastopol Street, Caulfield. Mindla adored her grandsons – but not enough to let them play in the good room. In fact, the only time they ever saw Nanna take the plastic off the sofa was when her friends Mrs Kuscinski, Mrs Snow and Mrs Fagelbaum came around to play cards. Mindla always told Mena she was her favourite daughter-in-law.

Gad passed away in 2017, and Mena in 2019.

Maks married Alina, and they gave Mindla and Kubush a precious granddaughter, Nerine, and another grandson, Ira. Whenever a circus came to town, Pop got tickets for the grandchildren to go along. Moscow Circus, Silvers Circus, Lennon Bros Circus, they've seen them all many times over. Nerine never wants to see a circus again!

Mindla always told Alina she was her favourite daughter-in-law.

Alina passed away in 1995 and Maks found happiness again with his partner Vicky.

Henry married Meg. Meg quickly learnt that when giving Mindla a gift, you always tucked the receipt inside the card, that way she could take the gift back when she didn't like it. Henry and Meg have two sons, Ralph (my husband) and Ben, who weren't allowed to play in the good room either. Nanna taught Ralph and Ben every Yiddish swear word they know.

Mindla always told Meg she was her favourite daughter-in-law.

Jadzia lived a long and happy life in Australia with Samuel and their adored daughter Hanna, who gave them the best gift of all, a precious granddaughter, Jessica, and a grandson, Jeremy. Jadzia passed away in 2004 aged 86. She was always welcomed into the good room (with the plastic *off*).

Faivel died in 1976 aged 70. He never married but was a well-known and much-loved member of the Jewish community in Caulfield and regularly attended the Moorabbin Shul. Faivel brought joy to many including his great-nieces, Debbie and Julie, who remember him fondly and were very generous with their time in the research of this book. He was a regular visitor to the Horowitz household.

He too was welcomed into the good room, but he much preferred to sit out in the back yard with Kubush, the sun on their backs and a glass of whisky in their hands. Oh, the tales they told. And we know them all, because David, Paul, Gad and Mena could hear every word over the back fence.

After World War II, Bronislaw Staniewski worked for the Polish National Circus. He and Lala cared for the women dwarves of the circus, building them a cottage on their property in the eastern Polish village of Milanow where the women lived out their days. Bronislaw died in 1956 aged 67. Lala Staniewska died in 1976. They are survived by a niece, Jolanta, and grandson, Mikolaj.

Between 23 July and 21 September 1942, an estimated 870,000 Jews were murdered at Treblinka. Mindla's father, Shmuel, and sisters Sonia, Shara and Minya were among them. The SS came at dawn, rounding up Jews to take to the newly established extermination camp. Eva and Laloshe were allowed to stay behind because they both had documents, importantly an Ausweis identity card permitting them to work, and Laloshe had a job at a factory making clothes for the Wehrmacht.

One by one the apartments at Muranowska were cleared out. Shmuel no doubt did his best to remain calm as he and his daughters Sonia, Minya and Shara silently merged with the tide of neighbours and friends headed for the railway line where cattle cars were waiting to transport them: men, women, children, pregnant women, the elderly. Some with babies in their arms and children on their backs. Some who'd not known a world without the Nazis, others whose wrinkles honoured years of survival; all bound for resettlement in the east.

Thousands of Jews were herded into the Umschlagplatz that day, a waiting area beside the main railway line. Late in the evening the cattle cars were loaded with human cargo, the doors and windows bolted tight behind them. When they arrived at Malkinia station, the driver uncoupled the first twenty boxcars of the sixty-car train and reversed them seven kilometres down a siding track into Treblinka. Ukrainian guards armed with truncheons and rifles hurried out the passengers. Once they were unloaded, the train driver was told to leave immediately, being strictly forbidden from entering Treblinka, a crime punishable by death. He returned to Malkinia to bring the next group of cattle cars. The camp was camouflaged by branches woven into a barbed-wire fence, with trees planted along the perimeter to deter prying eyes.

The new arrivals at Treblinka were told that the men would be sent to work and the women sent to the kitchen or laundry. All children would go to school. 'But first, you must all have a shower and be de-loused.'

As they passed the guards, each of the new arrivals was given a piece of string to lace their shoes together so they remained in pairs. With hundreds lined up for their showers, some might have assumed this was so their precious belongings didn't get mixed up.

The men were ordered to completely undress outside, while the women were herded into a barracks building and told to strip naked. Each woman had to have her head shaved and was then ushered outside, where one by one, they followed a barbed-wire enclosed path, disguised with trees, to the 'bathhouse'. The Germans had given this walkway to the gas chambers a name, Himmelfahrstrasse – the street to heaven. A Star of David was hung above the entrance and pot plants placed by the door, in mock decoration.

The shower building was designed so that only one person could enter at a time. It was impossible for the poor souls to turn back once they realised it was in fact a gas chamber.

Less than half an hour after they had arrived at Treblinka, every single person was dead.

For the next eight weeks, two transports per day arrived at Treblinka, one hundred and sixty cattle cars each day. It wasn't long before Eva and Laloshe made the fateful trip to Treblinka, too.

Each morning at sunrise a new train unloaded the living dead, a pattern followed all day and into the night.

It would have broken Mindla's heart to think of Sonia's beautiful long dark ponytail, along with Shara's blonde curls and Minya's brunette mane, shaved off and packed into bales that were then sold to German manufacturers. The women's hair was used to line car seats, make rope, weave carpet and stuff mattresses.

Mindla and Jadzia died believing that they were the only ones from the Levin family who survived the Holocaust, but in researching this book I discovered that two brothers recorded as 'perished' actually miraculously lived. Each brother planted roots on the opposite side of the world and raised a family, formed friendships, and built a life.

For the duration of the war, Yakov was detained in Soviet Union gulags at Yaroslavl and Rybinsky. After liberation he returned to Warsaw and searched for his family but found no trace. He settled in Israel, where he raised a family and lived a long life. He died in 2011 aged 89.

Menachem (known latterly as Mordtka) somehow survived the camps of Budzyn and Flossenbürg, where he made parts for the Nazis' Messerschmitt fighter aircraft, and Dachau, from which he was eventually liberated, albeit gravely ill with typhus. After the war he settled in the United States, where he raised two daughters with his wife, Juliana. In their later years, the family moved to Israel. Menachem and Yakov lived about a ten-minute drive from one another, never knowing of the other's existence, let alone that of two sisters a world away in Australia. The lost families have now connected and we endeavour to get to know one another and to slot the pieces of the family jigsaw puzzle together fully. I am particularly grateful to Yakov's daughter Hanna for her help.

It's heartbreaking to think that both brothers died believing they were the only survivor of their family; heartbreaking to think of the unspoken conversations, of birthdays, weddings and special occasions never shared. However, now that connections have been made with the families we never knew existed, our generation and all future ones will ensure their stories are told.

Mindla and Kubush loved Australia. Pop always called it 'the lucky country' and, just as he pledged on the day he arrived on these shores, he never left. 'Why would you ever go anywhere else?' he'd say.

With the help of Ernie Carroll, who sponsored them, Mindla and Kubush became Australian citizens. Ernie rose to fame as Ossie Ostrich on the popular show *Hey Hey It's Saturday*. Could anything be more Australian than having Ossie Ostrich sign their citizenship papers?

Mindla and Kubush lived for their grandchildren and great-grandchildren. Until his dying day, Pop never stopped entertaining. When his granddaughter, Nerine, was celebrating her fifth birthday, Pop arrived unexpectedly dressed in full clown regalia, face painted and costume on, much to the delight of his granddaughter and the horror of her parents.

As the guests moved to the back yard to feast on fairy bread and hot dogs, Pop put on a show.

Carrying a large plate covered in cake-shaped whipped cream, he tiptoed towards the birthday girl and, just as he had everyone's attention, tripped, planting his face smack bang in the middle of the cake. He was covered in cream from head to toe. The children laughed so hard their tummies hurt and Nerine thought it was the best birthday ever.

It was the last time Pop performed; his work was done.

ACKNOWLEDGEMENTS

In October 2018, while on assignment for *The Australian Women's Weekly*, I went on a river cruise in Budapest. As the boat prepared to set sail I chatted with a Sydney couple, Peter and Marika Lorschy. I had just been to the Shoes on the Danube Bank memorial, and had been deeply moved by the experience. It is no grand shrine or architectural monument, merely dozens of old shoes dotted along the river's edge just downstream from the parliament building: a child's tiny slipper, a much-loved pair of Mary Janes, a man's weathered workboots. Each shoe, modelled on an original pair and cast in iron for posterity, represents the 3500 people – 800 of them Jews – who were lined up along the riverbank during the 1944–45 winter, forced to take off their shoes, and then shot by the far-right Arrow Cross militia.

'I was there,' Marika said softly.

Her eyes told me she wasn't referring to the tourist crush that day.

293

In early 1944, she's not sure of the exact date, Marika was out with her father searching for food near their home when they came across a line of people with their backs to the river, facing a group of soldiers. They were ordered to remove their shoes, then shot, their bodies toppling backwards into the river as Marika and her father looked on in horror. The soldiers shooed the little girl and her father away in exchange for his gold watch. Thankfully their lives were spared, but what Marika witnessed that day would haunt her forever.

Over a glass of wine, I shared with Marika and Peter the story of Kubush and Mindla Horowitz, my grandparents-in-law, and how they too had survived the Holocaust.

'You must tell their story,' Marika insisted. 'Every story must be told.'

With Marika's encouraging voice in my ear, that evening I began writing, but this book would not have come to fruition without the help of many people who deserve far more praise than I can ever give them in these pages.

To Krystyna Duszniak, thank you. This book would not have been possible without your extraordinary skills in tracing the family history in Poland, uncovering documents and translating and interpreting them for me. Equally to your colleagues Anat Shem-or in Israel and Zosia Kusztal in Poland, without whom I would never have been able to put all of the pieces of the jigsaw together. None of us ever imagined that through the writing of this story we would uncover two families on opposite sides of the world.

One of the many remarkable discoveries on this journey was that David Landau, son of the owners of the Warsaw tannery where Nanna worked and the apartment building on Muranowska where the Levins lived, also made a new life in Australia. Thanks to Krystyna Duszniak, I was introduced to Miriam Mahemhoff, nee Landau, who was incredibly helpful in tracing Mindla's early years.

In Poland, Wojciech Kowalczyk and Janusz Sejbuk at the State School of Circus Art, Julinek. I am particularly grateful to Janusz for sharing his incredible knowledge of the history of the circus in Poland and so enthusiastically scouring the vast Polish circus archive for me. I will remember our visit to Julinek forever. To Jolanta Staniewska, niece of Bronislaw and Lala Staniewski, and Mikolaj Rogalinski, Lala's grandson, thank you for taking the time to speak with me.

To Marek Kawka for so patiently driving us around and translating during our visit to Poland. Thank you, Marek, we enjoyed your company enormously.

To the late Ron Blaskett who so enthusiastically recalled the days of *The Tarax Show* and his friendship with Pop, and to Norm Brown and Ernie Carroll for sharing treasured memories of a wonderful era of Australian television.

To Debbie Kopel and Julie Leder, nieces of Faivel. It was such a pleasure spending time with you, I am grateful of your memories and willingness to share them.

To Sue Hampel for faithfully reading the manuscript.

To Selwa Anthony for encouraging me to pursue this book, and to Sophie Ambrose and Louise Ryan at Penguin

Random House Australia for so enthusiastically embracing it. It very quickly became a much bigger project than any of us ever anticipated and I am especially grateful to Sophie for her care with the story, and her patience as each deadline passed and the manuscript wasn't delivered.

Enormous thanks to Clive Hebard for such a careful eye over copy and to proofreader Melissa Lane.

And lastly, of course, to the Horowitz family for all of their support and encouragement; to my wonderful parents-in-law, Meg and Henry, who welcomed me into the family with open arms and wholeheartedly encouraged me to write this story; and to David and Paul, Nerine, Maks and Vicky for sharing special memories, digging up old photographs and offering many funny recollections along the way. You all made this so much fun, thank you for supporting this project so enthusiastically.

Sadly Denis (Gad) and Mena passed away before the book was finished, but I am very grateful for the conversations we shared. They were both so gracious and generous with their time. I hope Denis is alive in the pages of this book.

To Hanna Brik-Levin, how wonderful to meet you! Thank you, Hanna, for sharing Yakov's story and becoming part of this journey and our lives.

And lastly to the ones who kicked off all of this. My husband Ralph, thoroughbred clown, whose memories of his adored Nanna and Zaidy always keep us amused.

And our children Charlie and Alexandra, because it was for them that this all began. Our desire to fully understand the family history so we could pass these stories on to their generation inspired the adventure of a lifetime.

We will never forget.

BIBLIOGRAPHY

Books

Ainsztein, Reuben, *Jewish Resistance in Nazi-occupied Eastern Europe: With a historical survey of the Jew as fighter and soldier in the Diaspora*, Elek, London, 1974.

Braithwaite, Rodric, *Moscow 1941: A city and its people at war*, Profile Books, London, 2006.

Czerniakow, Adam edited by Raul Hilberg, Stanislaw Staron, and Josef Kermisz, translated by Staron and the staff of Yad Vashem), *The Warsaw Diary of Adam Czerniakow: Prelude to doom*, Ivan R. Dee, Chicago, 1999.

Davies, Norman, *Trail of Hope: The Anders Army, an odyssey across three continents*, Osprey Publishing, Oxford, 2015.

Dekel, Mikhal, *Tehran Children: A Holocaust refugee odyssey*, W. W. Norton & Company, New York, 2019.

Dobroszycki, Lucjan and Barbara Kirshenblatt-Gimblett, *Image Before My Eyes: A photographic history of Jewish life in Poland before the Holocaust*, Schocken Books, New York, 1994.

Gilbert, Martin, *The Holocaust: The Jewish tragedy*, Harper-Collins, London, 1999.

Goldstein, Guta, *There Will Be Tomorrow: A memoir*, Makor Jewish Community Library, Caulfield South, 1999.

Greene, Joshua M. and Shiva Kumar (eds.), *Witness: Voices from the Holocaust*, Free Press, New York, 2001.

Gruener, Ruth, *Destined to Live: A true story of a child in the Holocaust*, Scholastic, New York, 2007.

Grunwald-Spier, Agnes, *Women's Experiences in the Holocaust: In their own words*, Amberley Publishing, Stroud, 2018.

Kaminska, Ruth Turkow, *Mink Coats and Barbed Wire*, Collins and Harvill, London, 1979.

Kelly, Catriona, *Children's World: Growing up in Russia, 1890–1991*, Yale University Press, New Haven, 2008.

Landau, David J., *Caged: A story of Jewish resistance*, Pan Macmillan, Sydney, 1999.

Lukacs, John, *June 1941: Hitler and Stalin*, Yale University Press, New Haven, 2007.

Manley, Rebecca, *To the Tashkent Station: Evacuation and survival in the Soviet Union at war*, Cornell University Press, Ithaca, 2009.

Mazzeo, Tilar J., *Irena's Children*, Simon & Schuster, London, 2017.

Neirick, Miriam, *When Pigs Could Fly and Bears Could Dance: A history of the Soviet circus*, University of Wisconsin Press, Madison, 2006.

Ofer, Dalia and Paula E. Hyman (eds.), *Jewish Women: A comprehensive historical encyclopedia*, University of Nebraska Press, Lincoln, 2007.

Opdyke, Irene Gut with Jennifer Armstrong, *In My Hands: Memories of a Holocaust rescuer*, Ember, New York, 1999.

Pinchuk, Ben-Cion, *Shtetl Jews Under Soviet Rule: Eastern Poland on the eve of the Holocaust*, Blackwell, Oxford, 1991.

Szereszewska, Helena, *Memoirs from Occupied Warsaw: 1940– 1945*, Vallentine Mitchell, London, 1997.

Zable, Arnold, *Jewels and Ashes*, Scribe, Melbourne, 1991.

Zwolski, Marcin, *Więzienie w Białymstoku w Latach 1912– 1944: Kartki z historii* [w:] *Społeczeństwo – wojsko – polityka. Studia i szkice ofiarowane Profesorowi Adamowi Czesławowi Dobrońskiemu z okazji 70 urodzin*, red. M. Dajnowicz, A. Miodowski, T. Wesolowski, Bialystok, 2013.

Journals

Goldlust, John, 'A Different Silence: The survival of more than 200,000 Polish Jews in the Soviet Union during World War II as a case study in cultural amnesia', *Australian Jewish Historical Society Journal*, vol. 21, part 1, November 2012, pp. 13–60.

Online resources

www.ekartkazwarszawy.pl – a website dedicated to the history of Warsaw with archival photos, eyewitness accounts and historical newspapers

www.jewishbialystok.pl – the website of the Museum of the Jews of Bialystok and the Region

www.jewishgen.org – Jewish genealogy website

www.jhi.pl/en/ringelblum-archive – the website of the Ringelblum Archive and the Emanuel Ringelblum Jewish Historical Institute, ul. Tlomackie 3/5, 00–090 Warsaw, Poland

www.ushmm.org – the website of the United States Holocaust Memorial Museum in Washington, DC, USA

www.yadvashem.org – the website of the World Holocaust Remembrance Center in Jerusalem, Israel

www.zapisyterroru.pl – Chronicles of Terror, a project organised and administered by the Witold Pilecki Institute of Solidarity and Valor in Warsaw, Poland

In addition I am enormously grateful to the following academics and historians who greatly assisted my research:

Sue Hampel OAM, Australian Centre for Jewish Civilization, Monash University

Julia Reichstein, Jewish Holocaust Centre, Melbourne

Maciej Wzorek, POLIN Museum of the History of Polish Jews, Warsaw

Lilianna Nalewajska, University of Warsaw Library, Warsaw

Anna Przybyszewska-Drozd, Jewish Historical Institute, Warsaw

Katarzyna (Kasia) Person, Ringelblum Archive, Jewish Historical Institute, Warsaw

Magdalena Kaleta, AST National Academy of Theatre Arts, Krakow

Dr Marcin Zwolski, Institute of National Remembrance, Bialystok

Danielle Willard-Kyle, Rutgers University, New Brunswick, New Jersey

Louise Micallef, Sir Louis Matheson Library, Monash University, Melbourne

Janelle Wilson, National Archives of Australia, Canberra

And Professor Norman Davies, who generously helped me piece together the jigsaw of Mindla and Kubush's journey with the Anders army.